SMART TAX STRATEGIES
FOR W-2 Earners

JULIO CLERVEAUX, EA, MBA

Title: Smart Tax Strategies for W-2 Earners

Author: Julio Clerveaux

Publisher: Clerveaux Publishing

Printed in the United States of America

First Edition

For media, bulk purchase inquiries, or permissions, please contact:

✉ info@W2TaxGuide.com

🌐 W2TaxGuide.com

Disclaimer

Dedication

To my wife, Phalone Clerveaux, your love, strength, and unwavering support make everything possible.

To my son, Emmanuel J. Clerveaux, and my daughters, Johana B. Clerveaux, Maeva Clerveaux, and Maliah Clerveaux, you are my greatest inspiration and the reason I strive for excellence every day. This book is for you.

To the memory of my parents, your sacrifices, values, and love continue to guide me in all that I do. I carry your legacy with pride and gratitude.

To my brothers and sisters, thank you for your love, encouragement, and the foundation of family that keeps me grounded.

A special shout-out to my brother, Eustache Clerveaux, Certified Financial Planner (CFP), Wealth Advisor, and fellow Enrolled Agent. Your example and guidance continue to inspire me.

And to all my friends, thank you for your support, wisdom, and belief in me throughout this journey.

Contents

Welcome to Smart Tax Strategies for W-2 Earners

Introduction

If you earn a paycheck and get a W-2 at the end of the year, this book is for you.

Why You Should Read This Book (Even If You Hate Taxes)

You might think tax planning is only for business owners or wealthy investors. The truth is, everyday employees have more control over their tax outcome than they realize. Whether you are single or married, early in your career, planning for retirement, raising a child, or paying off loans, some strategies can help you lower your tax bill and keep more of what you earn.

But no one hands you a guide when you get your first job. And most tax advice is either too basic or too complicated, which is why I wrote this book.

Smart Tax Strategies for W-2 Earners is designed to guide you through the tax-saving opportunities that apply to your specific situation. We will cover everything from choosing the right filing status and claiming credits to understanding employer benefits, investing wisely, and planning for major life events such as marriage, having children, or buying a home.

Each chapter includes clear explanations, real-life examples, and actionable tips. You will not need to memorize tax code or become a tax expert. The chapters ahead teach you what to look for and how to use the tools already available to you.

To get the most out of this book, start by reading Chapters 1 through 4, which cover the foundations of how taxes work. These chapters set the stage for everything that follows. Then, jump to the chapter that fits your filing status. For example, if you're filing as Head of Household, you can skip Chapters 5, 6, 7, and 9 and go directly to Chapter 8. Chapter 10 is only relevant if you have a side hustle. The remaining chapters cover tax strategies applicable to all filing statuses and are worth reading regardless of your situation.

If you have ever looked at your tax return and thought, "There has to be a better way," you are right. There is.

Let's get started.

Chapter One

What Gets Taxed and How: Wages, W-2s, and Tax Brackets Explained

Before we can understand how to read your W-2 or figure out your tax bracket, we need to start with the basics: What does the IRS tax? Not every dollar that flows into your bank account is treated equally. Some money is fully taxable, some is taxed later, and some may never be taxed at all. Knowing these differences is the first step to making sense of your W-2. Once you can distinguish between gross income, taxable income, and wages, you will understand how these numbers relate to each other and how they determine your position in the tax bracket system.

What Is Gross Income?

Gross income is the total income you receive in a year before any taxes, adjustments, or deductions are taken out. The IRS defines it as all income you receive in the form of money, goods, property, and services that is not exempt from tax. This includes wages, salaries, tips, bonuses, interest, dividends, rental income, business income, unemployment benefits, and certain retirement distributions. Gross income is the starting point for calculating your taxes. From this number, you subtract allowable adjustments to arrive at your adjusted gross income (AGI).

What Is Taxable Income?

The IRS defines taxable income as your gross income minus any adjustments and deductions you are allowed to claim. Gross income includes all income you receive in the form of money, goods, property, and services that are not exempt from tax, such as wages, salaries, tips, bonuses, interest, dividends, business income, rental income, and certain retirement distributions. From this total, you subtract adjustments (like IRA contributions or student loan interest) to get your adjusted gross income (AGI). You then subtract either the standard deduction or your itemized deductions to arrive at your taxable income. This is the amount the IRS uses to calculate your federal income tax.

What Are Wages?

For federal tax purposes, wages generally include all pay you receive from an employer for services you perform. This includes salaries, hourly pay, bonuses, commissions, tips, and certain taxable fringe benefits. Wages are reported in Box 1 of your W-2 and form the largest part of most people's taxable income. Some amounts you receive from your employer, such as contributions to a traditional 401(k) or pre-tax health insurance premiums, are excluded from Box 1 and are not subject to federal income tax in the year contributed.

What Is a W-2 Form?

A W-2 is the IRS form employers use to report annual wages and the amount of taxes withheld from your paycheck. Every employer who pays an employee $600 or more in a calendar year is required to provide a W-2 to that employee. This form is the primary document used when filing federal and state income taxes, and each box contains specific information. Understanding each box is crucial to maximizing the benefits of the tax codes.

Understanding Key Boxes on the W-2

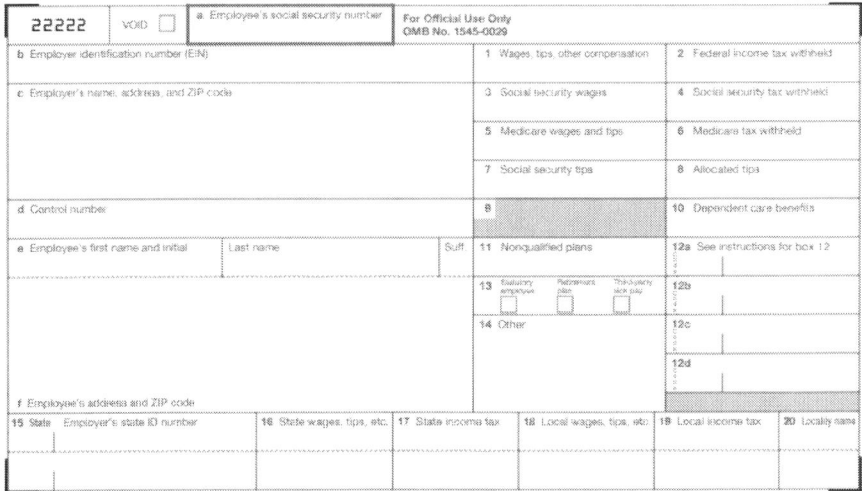

Figure 1

W-2 Box Reference Table

Box	What It Shows	Why It Matters
1	Wages, tips, and other taxable compensation, excluding pre-tax deductions (like health insurance, HSA, or 401(k) contributions).	This is the starting point for calculating your federal taxable income, which is usually lower than your gross pay.
2	Total federal income tax withheld.	Shows how much you have already paid toward your federal tax bill.

3	Social Security wages, subject to tax up to the annual limit.	Determines how much of your earnings are subject to Social Security tax.
4	6.2% of the wages in Box 3.	Confirms Social Security tax withheld, which should stop once the annual limit is reached.
5	Medicare wages and tips, with no wage cap.	All wages are subject to Medicare tax, unlike Social Security.
6	1.45% of Box 5, plus 0.9% surtax for high earners ($125k MFS, $250k MFJ, $200k others).	Ensures correct Medicare tax, including the surtax if your income is above the threshold.
7	Social Security tips.	Tips are taxable for Social Security, even if not in your base wages.
8	Allocated tips (not in Box 1).	You must include these on your tax return, as no withholding has been taken.
9	Obsolete; formerly tracked Advance EIC payments.	No longer used, but may appear on older W-2s.
10	Employer-provided dependent care benefits (up to $5,000 tax-free).	Reduces taxable income if benefits qualify.

11	Distributions from nonqualified deferred compensation plans.	May be fully taxable; requires careful reporting.
12	Various codes (e.g., Code C for taxable group-term life insurance, Code D for 401(k) contributions).	Each code affects how income or benefits are taxed.
13	Checkboxes: statutory employee, retirement plan participant, third-party sick pay.	Impacts eligibility for deductions and credits.
14	Miscellaneous employer information (union dues, after-tax contributions, uniform allowances).	Helpful for state returns or personal recordkeeping.
15–20	State and local wages, taxes withheld, and the Employer's state ID number.	Needed to file state or local tax returns.

How The Tax Bracket Works

The U.S. has a progressive tax system, so your income is taxed at multiple rates. This means that as your income grows, the next dollar above a certain amount is taxed at a higher rate. Only the income within a given bracket is taxed at the rate applicable to that bracket. For example, if you're married, filing jointly, and earn $150,000, only a portion of your income is taxed at higher rates, not the entire amount. Additionally, the income limits for all filers are adjusted annually for inflation. For the tax year 2025, the top tax rate is 37% for individual single taxpayers with incomes greater than $626,350 ($751,600 for married couples filing jointly). The One Big Beautiful Bill Act (OBBBA) repealed the 2025 sunset for TCJA provisions, so the 37% bracket stays in place.

2025 Tax Brackets and Federal Income Tax Rates | Tax Foundation

Tax Rate	For Single Filers	For Married Individuals Filing Joint Returns	For Heads of Households
10%	$0 to $11,925	$0 to $23,850	$0 to $17,000
12%	$11,925 to $48,475	$23,850 to $96,950	$17,000 to $64,850
22%	$48,475 to $103,350	$96,950 to $206,700	$64,850 to $103,350
24%	$103,350 to $197,300	$206,700 to $394,600	$103,350 to $197,300
32%	$197,300 to $250,525	$394,600 to $501,050	$197,300 to $250,500
35%	$250,525 to $626,350	$501,050 to $751,600	$250,500 to $626,350
37%	$626,350 or more	$751,600 or more	$626,350 or more

Figure 2

Marginal vs. Effective Tax Rate

The marginal tax rate is the rate you pay on your next dollar of income, while the effective tax rate is the average rate you pay on your total taxable income. For example, if you are a single filer in 2025 with $75,000 in taxable income, your marginal rate is 22%, because that's the highest bracket your income falls into. But you don't pay 22% on the entire $75,000. Instead, your income is taxed in layers: 10% on the first $11,925, 12% on the next $36,550, and 22% on the remaining $26,525. After adding up the tax on each portion, your total federal income tax would be approximately $11,414, resulting in an effective tax rate of roughly 15.22%, which is lower than your marginal rate.

Withholding

Withholding is the amount of federal and State income tax that your employer deducts from your paycheck throughout the year and sends directly to the IRS on your behalf. It is based on the information you provide on your Form W-4, including your filing status, dependents, and any additional income or deductions you expect to claim. The goal of withholding is to pay your tax liability

15

gradually for the year, rather than all at once when you file your return. If too much is withheld, you may get a refund when you file; if too little is withheld, you may owe money and possibly face penalties. For example, if you earn $75,000 in taxable income and your W-4 is completed accurately, your employer will withhold a portion of each paycheck based on the IRS withholding tables for the year. It's essential to review your withholding at least once a year, or whenever you experience a life change, such as getting married or having a child, to ensure the correct amount is being withheld.

From Paystub to W-2: What to Review Before Filing Your Taxes

Most people receive paychecks on a weekly or biweekly basis, and each time, the employer issues a pay stub. This document outlines the details of your earnings and deductions for the specific pay period. It shows how much you have earned before taxes (your gross pay), what has been deducted for federal and state taxes, Social Security, Medicare, retirement plans, and other benefits. Over time, these pay stubs form a financial timeline of your year at work. Your final paystub of the year, often referred to as the year-end snapshot, is particularly important because it summarizes your total earnings and withholdings for the year. It also serves as a preview of your W-2 form, which your current and/or former employer is required to send by January 31st of the following year.

Your W-2 is one of the most important documents for filing your federal and state tax returns. You will use it to complete Form 1040, report wages, and claim withholdings, deductions, and credits. Many employers issue W-2s electronically, and the IRS matches your return to what your employer reports. If your W-2 and tax return do not match, your return could be delayed or flagged for review. That's why it's essential to compare your W-2 with your final paystub and ensure all the information is accurate.

Common mistakes can easily lead to filing errors, which ultimately can cost you money. People often assume all income is taxed at their highest rate, when in reality, only the income in the top bracket is taxed at that rate. Others skip Box 12, missing key details about pre-tax retirement contributions that lower taxable income. There is also confusion between Medicare wages in Box 5 and taxable income in Box 1, which can differ due to pre-tax deductions. Lastly, many overlook Box 17, which reports state and local tax withholdings. Taking the time to review your W-2 and final paystub side by side can help you avoid these common pitfalls and file a more accurate return.

Action Steps for W-2 Earners

As a W-2 earner, a few simple habits can help you stay on top of your tax situation and avoid surprises at filing time. First, review your W-2 each year for accuracy, especially Boxes 1, 3, 5, and 12, as errors in these fields can affect your refund or result in notices from the IRS. If you consistently receive a large refund or owe money when filing, take a closer look at your withholding and adjust your W-4 with your employer. Generally, a large refund is not a good thing, as it means that you are lending the Government money for free. Next, track your pre-tax deductions, such as health insurance premiums, retirement contributions, and flexible spending account payments, to understand how they affect your taxable income and ensure you are maximizing the benefits available through your workplace. Finally, consult with a tax professional such as a CPA or an enrolled agent if you are unsure how to read your W-2 or if your tax situation becomes more complex. A professional can help you interpret the form correctly and make informed decisions for the year ahead.

Final Thoughts on Chapter One

Understanding your W-2 and how the tax brackets work is one of the most important first steps you can take toward smarter tax planning. This form is more than just a summary of your income; it is a window into how your money is taxed, how much has already been paid to the IRS, and what opportunities you may have to adjust and improve your financial position. By paying attention to the details in your pay stubs, knowing what each box on your W-2 means, and understanding how your income is taxed in brackets, you put yourself in a much stronger position come tax time. Whether your goal is to avoid underpayment penalties, get a more accurate refund, or gain clarity over your financial picture, it all starts with understanding the numbers in front of you.

Next, we will explore filing status, one of the most important yet often overlooked decisions you make when preparing your tax return. Your filing status affects your standard deduction, tax bracket, eligibility for credits, and even whether you qualify for certain deductions. Choosing the right status can make a significant difference in your tax outcome, so it is worth taking the time to understand how it works.

Chapter Two
Filing Status – Getting It Right from the Start

Your filing status is one of the most important choices you make when preparing your tax return. It determines your standard deduction, your tax brackets, the forms you use, and whether you qualify for valuable tax credits. It also affects the amount of tax you owe or the amount you receive back. Sounds simple, but many taxpayers choose the wrong status or overlook a better one, often leaving money on the table.

Tax Pro Tip: Choosing the right filing status can unlock credits like the Earned Income Tax Credit (EITC) and the Child Tax Credit (CTC). Review eligibility each year if your family situation changes.

There are five filing statuses under the U.S. tax code. Choosing the right one depends on your marital status, family situation, and who you financially support.

Filing Status Comparison Chart (2025)

Filing Status	2024 Standard Deduction	2025 Standard Deduction	Who Can Use It	Key Benefits	Common Limitations
Single	$14,600	$15,750	Unmarried individuals without dependents	Simple filing process, base tax rates	Lower deductions and tighter brackets

					than other statuses
Married Filing Jointly	$29,200	$31,500	Legally married couples filing one combined return	Widest tax brackets, access to most tax credits	Both spouses are entirely liable for taxes and accuracy
Married Filing Separately	$14,600	$15,750	Married couples filing separate returns	May protect a refund from a spouse's debt	Many credits and deductions become limited or unavailable
Head of Household	$21,900	$23,625	Unmarried individuals who support a qualifying dependent and pay over half of the costs	Higher deduction than Single, better brackets	Must pay more than half of the household expenses and have a dependent
Qualifying Widow(er)	$29,200	$31,500	Widows or widowers with a dependent child, in the two years following a spouse's death	Retains Married Filing Jointly benefits for two years	Only available for two years; must not remarry during this period

Figure 3

Single Filing Status

This is the most straightforward status. If you're unmarried, divorced, or legally separated on the last day of the year and don't qualify for any other status, this is your default.

Example: Jeff is twenty-seven years old, single, and works as a graphic designer. He lives alone and doesn't support anyone else financially. His status is Single.

The Single status comes with the lowest standard deduction, which is $15,750 and indexed for inflation, and narrower tax brackets compared to other statuses. While it's simple, it may not be the most favorable if you have a qualifying child or support a relative. In that case, you might be eligible for Head of Household, which we'll cover shortly.

Married Filing Jointly (MFJ)

If you're married as of December 31st, you can file jointly with your spouse. This status combines your income and deductions into a single return, typically resulting in a lower tax liability. It also opens the door to more tax credits and deductions, including the Earned Income Tax Credit (EITC), education credits, and IRA deductions. The One Big Beautiful Bill Act (OBBBA) increases the base standard deduction amounts for married taxpayers filing jointly (MFJ) beginning in tax year 2025 to $31,500, which is also indexed for inflation.

Example: Sarah and Mike plan to get married in December 2025. Even though they were single most of the year, they will be considered married for the entire tax year and can file jointly. Doing so increases their standard deduction for the 2025 tax year to $31,500, allowing them to access wider tax brackets.

MFJ is usually the most favorable status for married couples, but there are exceptions, especially if one spouse has complex tax issues, such as back taxes or defaulted student loans.

Married Filing Separately (MFS)

Married couples can choose to file separately, but it's rarely beneficial. Filing separately may be beneficial in specific legal or financial situations, such as protecting one spouse from liability or keeping income-based loan repayments low; however, many credits and deductions phase out or become unavailable when filing separately. The base standard deduction amount for married taxpayers filing separately (MFS) beginning in tax year 2025 is the same as the standard deduction for single filers, which is $15,750, indexed for inflation.

Example: Joan and Jorge are married, but Jorge has defaulted on federal student loans. If they file jointly, the IRS could take their refund to cover Jorge's debt. To avoid this, they decide to file separately. While Joan loses access to some credits, she avoids having her refund withheld.

In general, MFS should only be used if there's a compelling legal or financial reason. Otherwise, MFJ typically results in lower overall tax.

Watch Out: Married Filing Separately (MFS) usually disqualifies you from credits such as the EITC, Child and Dependent Care Credit, and education credits.

Head of Household (HOH)

This status offers a higher standard deduction and more favorable tax brackets than filing Single. The base standard deduction amount for the Head of Household (HOH) filing status, effective in tax year 2025, is $23,625, indexed for inflation. To qualify, you must be unmarried, pay more than half the cost of maintaining your home, and have a qualifying dependent who resides with you for more than half the year.

Example: Jasmine is a single mother with a six-year-old son. She pays the rent, utilities, and all other household expenses. She qualifies as the Head of Household, which reduces her tax bill and increases her eligibility for credits, such as the Child Tax Credit.

A common mistake is thinking you qualify as HOH just because you have a child. The key is that you must pay more than half of the household costs and have a qualifying dependent who lives with you most of the year.

Qualifying Widow(er) with Dependent Child

If your spouse died in the past two years and you have a dependent child, you may be able to use this status. It allows you to use the same standard deduction and tax brackets as Married Filing Jointly, which can offer significant tax savings.

Example: Jimmy's wife passed away in 2023. He's raising their eight-year-old daughter and pays all household expenses. For both 2024 and 2025, Jimmy can file as a Qualifying Widower with a Dependent Child, which will give him the same benefits as if he were still married and filing jointly.

To qualify, you must have a dependent child and not have remarried before the end of the year. After two years, you'll need to switch to Head of Household or Single, depending on your situation.

Filing Status Decision Table

Question	If YES	If NO
1. Were you married on December 31st?	Go to Question 2	Go to Question 5
2. Will you and your spouse file jointly?	Married Filing Jointly (MFJ)	Go to Question 3
3. Did your spouse die during the year?	MFJ for this year. Go to Question 4 for future years	Married Filing Separately (MFS)
4. Did your spouse die within the last 2 years, and do you have a dependent child?	Qualifying Surviving Spouse (QSS)	Go to Question 5
5. Did you pay more than half the cost of keeping up your home and have a qualified dependent?	Head of Household (HOH)	Single

Notes:

➢ A qualified dependent generally means a child or relative who lived with you for more than half the year.

➢ You are considered unmarried for HOH purposes if your spouse did not live with you for the last 6 months of the year and you meet other support tests.

➢ A Qualifying Surviving Spouse must have a dependent child and meet MFJ requirements in the year of the spouse's death.

If you're still unsure, consult a tax professional who can assess your situation and advise you on the most favorable option.

Changing Filing Status

Your filing status can change from one year to the next depending on life events. Marriage, divorce, separation, or the death of a spouse can all shift your eligibility. Don't assume last year's status still applies; continually reassess before filing.

Example: Louise filed as Married Filing Jointly in 2023, but she and her spouse finalized a divorce in December 2024. She now lives with her two children and pays all household expenses. For 2024, she qualifies for Head of Household, not Single.

Impact on Deductions and Credits

Your filing status determines your standard deduction and your income tax bracket. It also affects whether you qualify for valuable credits like the Child Tax Credit, Earned Income Tax Credit, the American Opportunity and Lifetime Learning Credits, and the Saver's Credit. You may be able to deduct up to $2,500 in student loan interest, contribute to a 401(k) or IRA to lower your taxable income, and use an HSA or FSA to set aside pre-tax dollars for medical expenses. Educators can deduct out-of-pocket classroom expenses, including costs for coaches and health instructors. These options provide W-2 workers with practical tools to reduce their tax burden, even if they don't itemize their deductions or operate a business.

Temporary New Tax Breaks with Big Impact

The One Big Beautiful Bill Act (OBBBA), signed into law on July 4th, 2025, makes several significant changes to the federal tax code for tax years 2025 through 2028. It creates a deduction of up to $25,000 per year for qualified tip income, allowing service workers to reduce their taxable income if tips are correctly reported and tied to specific jobs such as servers, bartenders, or bellhops. Starting in 2025, W-2 employees may deduct up to $12,500 of qualified overtime wages per person, or $25,000 for married couples filing jointly. Overtime wages must meet the IRS definition of "qualified overtime," which refers to hours worked beyond 40 in a week, paid at a rate of at least one and a half times the regular rate. The deduction reduces both taxable income and adjusted gross income (AGI). Social Security and Medicare taxes still apply. The deduction phases out once MAGI exceeds $150,000 for single/HOH filers or $300,000 for joint filers. This provision expires after 2028. However, Married Filing Separate (MFS) filers will not be eligible for these two deductions. Additionally, there is a new charitable deduction available to non-itemizers: up to $1,000 if you're single or $2,000 if married filing jointly, as long as your total giving exceeds 0.5% of your income. The bill also introduces a new $6,000 senior deduction for taxpayers aged sixty-five and over, as well as for spouses who are also sixty-five if filing jointly. This deduction phases out at higher income levels and requires the reporting of a Social Security number. Finally, for vehicles purchased between 2025 and 2028, interest on personal-use car loans is deductible up to $10,000 per year. To qualify, the vehicle must be brand new, assembled in the United States, and financed with a first-lien secured loan. The vehicle must be used strictly for personal purposes and not for business activity. This deduction is temporary and will sunset after 2028.

Common Mistakes When Choosing a Filing Status

- Filing Single when you qualify for Head of Household
- Filing Married Filing Jointly when you are legally separated
- Forgetting to change your status after a divorce or the death of a spouse

- Filing Married Filing Separately without understanding the tax trade-offs

These mistakes are more common than you'd think and can result in IRS audits, penalties, or missed refunds.

Final Thoughts on Filing Status

Your filing status is not just a box you check; it affects nearly every line of your tax return. Choosing the right one can reduce your tax bill, increase your refund, and unlock valuable credits. Review your situation annually, especially if your life circumstances have changed. When in doubt, speak with a tax professional. Getting this one detail right can make all the difference.

Chapter Three

Introduction to Tax Deductions – Keep More of What You Earn

Tax deductions are one of the most effective tools W-2 earners can use to lower their tax bill. Whether you are a salaried employee working one job or multiple jobs, understanding deductions helps you make smarter financial decisions throughout the year, not just when it's time to file.

At the most basic level, a tax deduction reduces your taxable income, which in turn reduces the amount of income tax you owe. The more deductions you qualify for, the less income the IRS can tax you. That means more of your money stays in your pocket.

There are two primary methods for claiming deductions: taking the standard deduction or itemizing your deductions using Schedule A. You can only choose one, not both, so choosing the right approach can make a noticeable difference in your refund or tax bill.

What Is the Standard Deduction?

The standard deduction is a fixed amount that the IRS allows you to subtract from your taxable income. You don't have to track expenses, save receipts, or fill out extra forms; simply check the box, subtract the amount, and proceed. See Figure 3 for the tax year 2025 standard deduction. Please note that these numbers typically increase annually due to inflation.

Example: Melissa is single with no mortgage, no major medical bills, and no significant donations. Her eligible expenses only total

$6,000. Since the standard deduction is more than twice that amount, it makes sense for her to take the standard deduction of $15,750 for the tax year 2025 and skip itemizing altogether.

Who Should Take the Standard Deduction?

Most taxpayers take the standard deduction. According to the IRS, about 87% of filers claimed the standard deduction in 2018, and the Tax Policy Center reports that figure rose to roughly 90% in more recent years. If your itemizable deductions are less than your standard deduction, you'll usually save more by claiming the standard deduction. It's simpler, faster, and requires no documentation. This is especially true for renters, younger taxpayers, and those without significant medical or charitable expenses.

However, if you own a home, donate significantly to charity, or have high out-of-pocket medical costs, it's worth checking whether itemizing your deductions could lower your tax bill.

What Are Itemized Deductions?

Itemized deductions allow you to subtract specific, qualified expenses from your income, but they require more work and documentation. You will need to list your expenses on Schedule A, keep supporting documents, and meet certain thresholds to deduct some categories.

Itemizing can result in a lower tax bill but only if your total deductions exceed the standard deduction. Note that if you're married and filing separately, you can't take the standard deduction if your spouse itemizes. You must both choose the same method. Below are some common examples of qualified expenses that can reduce your tax liabilities.

Medical and Dental Expenses

You can only deduct unreimbursed medical expenses above 7.5% of your adjusted gross income (AGI).

Example: If your AGI is $100,000, you can only deduct medical costs that exceed $7,500. If you spent $10,000 out of pocket, only $2,500 would count as a deduction.

This often helps older taxpayers or those with high healthcare costs, especially in years with major surgeries, long-term care, or out-of-network treatments.

State and Local Taxes (SALT)

Starting in tax year 2025, you can deduct up to $40,000 in combined property taxes, state income taxes, and sales taxes if you're married filing jointly. If your tax filing status is 'married filing separately' (MFS), the cap is $20,000. These limits begin to phase out once your adjusted gross income exceeds $500,000 for all filers except for MFS, which is $250,000. The deduction limits will increase by 1% each year through 2029, then return to $10,000 in 2030.

Mortgage Interest and PMI Deduction

You can deduct mortgage interest on up to $750,000 of mortgage debt if the loan was taken out after December 15th, 2017. This applies to your primary residence and one additional home. Under the One Big Beautiful Bill Act, this $750,000 limit is now permanent. The law also permanently restores the deduction for private mortgage insurance (PMI), treating it as qualified residence interest beginning with tax year 2026.

Example: Djouly plans to buy her first home in 2026 with a $600,000 mortgage and pay PMI. She can deduct the full interest expense on the loan along with her PMI payments, which may make itemizing more beneficial, especially in the early years of the mortgage when these costs are highest.

> **Note:** The $750,000 cap applies per return, not per individual. Married couples filing jointly share the same $750,000 limit, while two single filers could each deduct interest on up to $750,000 of mortgage debt. This creates a marriage penalty for couples buying property together, since their combined deduction may be less than if they had purchased separately and filed as single taxpayers.

Charitable Contributions

You can deduct cash donations to qualified nonprofits up to 60% of your AGI. Non-cash contributions, such as clothing or household items, must be documented and may have lower donation limits. Under the 2025 tax law changes, filers who do not itemize may now claim an above-the-line deduction for qualified charitable contributions. The deduction is limited to $1,000 for single filers and $2,000 for married couples filing jointly, and it applies to cash donations made to eligible 501(c)(3) organizations. While itemizing may still provide a larger benefit, this new rule ensures that taxpayers who take the standard deduction can still reduce taxable income for charitable giving.

Pro Tip: Always get a receipt or confirmation letter from the non-profit organization. The IRS does not accept estimates, and vague records can result in an audit and ultimately disallowed deductions.

Other Important Deductions

Several valuable deductions continue to apply to W-2 earners. The educator expense deduction remains in place and has been expanded to include more roles, such as coaches, interscholastic program staff, and health or physical education instructors. This deduction continues to apply whether or not you itemize, and can be claimed under Section 162 starting in 2025. Capital gains may be deferred or reduced by investing in Qualified Opportunity Funds, which now have updated holding rules and increased incentives for investments in low-income communities or rural zones. Homeowners may exclude up to $250,000 ($500,000 if married filing jointly) in gain on the sale of a primary residence if the ownership and use tests are met. Gambling losses remain deductible up to the amount of documented winnings. Finally, Losses from both federally and state-declared disasters are now deductible, as long as the loss exceeds 10% of your AGI and isn't covered by insurance.

Comparing Standard and Itemized: Which Is Better?

There is no one-size-fits-all answer. The best approach is to estimate your total itemized deductions and compare them to the standard deduction. If itemizing gives you a larger deduction, it is worth the extra effort.

Work with your tax advisor to run both scenarios side by side to compare the results. That's what professionals do, and it could easily save you hundreds or even thousands of dollars.

Standard Deduction vs. Itemized Deductions

Category	Standard Deduction	Itemized Deductions
Definition	Fixed amount set by the IRS based on filing status	Actual qualified expenses you report on Schedule A
2025 Deduction Amounts	- Single: $15,750 - Head of Household: $23,625 - Married Filing Jointly: $31,500	Varies depending on actual expenses (no fixed amount)
Documentation Required	No receipts or expense tracking needed	Requires receipts, proof of payment, and detailed records
Best For	Most taxpayers with simple finances or lower deductible expenses	Taxpayers with high mortgage interest, medical costs, state taxes, or charitable giving
Common Mistakes	Assuming you cannot qualify for credits if you take the standard deduction	Overestimating deductions, missing documentation, or claiming ineligible expenses

Tax Planning Tip: Bunching Deductions

If your itemized deductions are close to the standard deduction threshold, consider bunching deductible expenses into a single year.

Example: Let's say you usually donate $5,000 per year to charity and pay $8,000 in property taxes. If you double your charitable giving in one year and skip it the next, you might push your deductions over the standard limit for that year. This way, you itemize one year and take the standard deduction the next, maximizing benefits over two years.

Common Mistakes When Itemizing

- Forgetting to include property taxes or deducting only mortgage interest
- Overestimating charitable deductions without having written proof
- Claiming ineligible medical expenses, such as cosmetic surgery or over-the-counter items
- Not realizing that high income may phase out certain itemized deductions in the future (if the law changes)

Changes to Deduction Rules in Recent Tax Laws

Taking the standard deduction doesn't disqualify you from claiming some tax credits. You can still receive the Child Tax Credit, the Earned Income Tax Credit, and education credits such as the American Opportunity Credit or Lifetime Learning Credit. Deductions reduce your taxable income, while credits reduce your actual tax bill, and some are even refundable. Recent tax law changes, including the Tax Cuts and Jobs Act of 2017 and the Tax One Big Beautiful Bill Act, significantly changed deduction rules by increasing the standard deduction and suspending many miscellaneous itemized deductions. In addition to legislative changes, annual inflation adjustments affect deduction thresholds. As a result, whether it makes sense to itemize or take the standard deduction can vary from year to year. Staying in touch with a qualified tax advisor, such as a CPA or an enrolled agent, can help ensure you make informed decisions and avoid costly mistakes.

Final Thoughts on Chapter 3

Choosing between the standard deduction and itemizing is more than just a filing step; it's a financial decision that can impact your refund, tax liability, and even your tax planning for next year. Each tax season is an opportunity to reflect on what changed in your life: Did you buy a house? Have surgery? Make a large donation? These events can swing the balance in favor of itemizing.

Evaluate your situation annually, review the numbers, and utilize the available tools to make the most tax-smart decision. And when you're not sure, ask a professional. That one decision might save you more than you think.

Chapter Four

Introduction to Tax Credits – Dollar-for-Dollar Savings on Your Tax Bill

Tax credits are one of the most powerful ways W-2 earners can lower their tax bill. While deductions reduce your taxable income, credits directly reduce the amount of tax you owe. In some cases, credits can even increase your refund if they are refundable. Understanding how credits work and which ones you qualify for can have a significant impact on your final tax outcome.

At the most basic level, a tax credit is a dollar-for-dollar reduction of your tax liability. If you owe $3,000 in taxes and you have a $1,000 credit, your tax bill drops to $2,000. This makes credits especially valuable because their impact is not diluted by your tax bracket, unlike deductions.

Types of Tax Credits

Refundable credits can reduce your tax liability below zero, allowing you to receive a refund even if you owe no tax. For example, the Earned Income Tax Credit (EITC) and the Additional Child Tax Credit.

Nonrefundable credits can reduce your tax bill to zero but will not generate a refund for any unused portion. For Example, the Lifetime Learning Credit, the Saver's Credit.

Both types can play an important role in your tax plan. Many credits also have income limits, phaseouts, or other eligibility requirements, so knowing the rules is essential.

Family and Dependent Credits:

The Child Tax Credit (CTC)

The Child Tax Credit (CTC) is a valuable tax benefit for families with dependent children under age seventeen. For the 2025 tax year, the credit is worth up to $2,200 per qualifying child, with up to $1,700 of that amount being refundable. This means that if your tax liability is less than the credit, you may still receive a portion of it as a refund. The credit begins to phase out at higher income levels: $400,000 for married couples filing jointly and $200,000 for single or head-of-household filers. For example, a family with two children under 17 who qualify for the full credit could reduce their tax bill by $4,400. If their tax liability is less than that amount, they may still receive up to $3,400 in refundable credit. The CTC helps lower your tax burden and can provide a significant refund for eligible families, making it one of the most effective tax tools for W-2 earners with children.

Additional Child Tax Credit

The Additional Child Tax Credit (ACTC) is a refundable credit designed to help families who do not owe enough income tax to claim the full Child Tax Credit (CTC). For the 2025 tax year, up to $1,700 per qualifying child may be refundable through the ACTC. This means that even if your tax bill is zero, you may still receive a refund based on your earned income and the number of qualifying children. To be eligible, you must have at least $2,500 of earned income, and the refund amount is generally calculated as 15% of your income above that threshold, up to the maximum limit. For example, if you qualify for the CTC but only owe $500 in taxes, and you have two children, you could still receive up to $3,900 back as a refund through the ACTC. This credit provides essential support for lower and moderate-income families by helping them access a portion of the CTC even without a significant tax liability.

Credit for Other Dependents

The Credit for Other Dependents is a nonrefundable credit of up to $500 per qualifying dependent who does not qualify for the Child Tax Credit. This includes older children aged seventeen and above, elderly parents, or other relatives, as well as non-relatives who live with you and receive more than half of their financial support from you. The dependent must be a U.S. citizen, national, or resident alien, and they must have a valid taxpayer identification number. The credit begins to phase out at the same income levels as the CTC: $400,000 for married couples filing jointly and $200,000 for single or head-of-household filers. While not refundable, this credit still helps reduce your tax bill and provides additional support for households caring for adult dependents or extended family members.

Child and Dependent Care Credit

The Child and Dependent Care Credit helps working taxpayers cover the cost of care for a child under age thirteen or a disabled spouse or dependent while they work or look for work. For the 2025 tax year, you may claim up to 35% of $3,000 in expenses for one dependent, or $6,000 for two or more dependents. This results in a maximum credit of $1,050 or $2,100, respectively. Eligible expenses include daycare, after-school programs, and in-home care providers. To qualify, the care must be provided so you can work or actively look for work, and the provider cannot be your spouse, a parent of the child, or a dependent on your return. While the credit is nonrefundable, it directly reduces your tax bill and can offer meaningful relief for working families who pay out-of-pocket for caregiving expenses.

The Earned Income Tax Credit (EITC)

The Earned Income Tax Credit (EITC) is a refundable credit designed to support low to moderate-income workers. The credit amount depends on your earned income, filing status, and number of qualifying children. Even workers without children may qualify, though the benefit is larger for those with dependents. For 2025, a single filer with two children earning under $50,000 could receive a credit of more than $5,500. To be eligible, you must have earned income below specific limits and meet residency and filing requirements. You must also be at least twenty-five years old and under sixty-five if claiming the credit without children. Additionally, you cannot claim the EITC if your investment income exceeds the limit, which is $11,000 for 2025. Because the EITC is refundable, you can receive the full credit even if your tax liability is zero, making it one of the most effective tools for boosting after-tax income for eligible workers.

Education Credits:

American Opportunity Tax Credit (AOTC)

The American Opportunity Tax Credit (AOTC) is a valuable education credit worth up to $2,500 per eligible student for the first four years of postsecondary education. It covers qualified expenses such as tuition, required fees, and course materials. Up to 40% of the credit, or $1,000, is refundable, meaning you can receive that portion even if you owe no tax. To qualify, the student must be enrolled at least half-time in a program leading to a degree or credential, and cannot have finished the first four years of college. The credit phases out for single filers with a modified adjusted gross income above $80,000 and joint filers with a modified adjusted gross income above $160,000. For example, if you pay $4,000 in qualified expenses, you may be able to claim the full $2,500 credit. The AOTC can significantly reduce your tax liability or increase your refund, making it one of the most beneficial tax breaks for W-2 earners with college students in the household.

Lifetime Learning Credit (LLC)

The Lifetime Learning Credit (LLC) offers a nonrefundable credit of up to $2,000 per tax return for qualified tuition and related expenses paid for postsecondary education. Unlike the American Opportunity Tax Credit, the LLC has no limit on the number of years it can be claimed and is available for part-time students, graduate programs, and continuing education courses. The credit equals 20% of the first $10,000 in eligible expenses, making it particularly beneficial for adults returning to school or enhancing their skills. For example, if you pay $3,000 for part-time continuing education, you may be eligible for a $600 credit. Income limits apply, with the credit beginning to phase out for single filers with a modified adjusted gross income (MAGI) of more than $80,000 and joint filers with a MAGI of more than $160,000. Because the LLC is nonrefundable, it can reduce your tax liability to zero, but it cannot generate a refund. It remains a valuable tax benefit for W-2 earners looking to advance their careers or gain new credentials through ongoing education.

Retirement and Savings Incentives

Saver's Credit

The Saver's Credit is a nonrefundable tax credit that rewards low- to moderate-income taxpayers for contributing to retirement accounts, such as 401(k)s, Traditional IRAs, and Roth IRAs. For the 2025 tax year, the credit is worth up to $1,000 for single filers and $2,000 for married couples filing jointly. The amount of the credit is 10%, 20%, or 50% of your retirement contributions, depending on your adjusted gross income and filing status. To qualify, you must be at least eighteen years old, not claimed as a dependent on someone else's return, and not a full-time student. For example, a single filer who earns $20,000 and contributes $2,000 to a Traditional IRA could receive a $1,000 credit, reducing their tax bill dollar for dollar. The Saver's Credit is often overlooked but can be a powerful incentive for W-2 earners to build retirement savings while lowering their current-year tax liability.

ABLE Account Saver's Credit

Suppose you contribute to an ABLE (Achieving a Better Life Experience) account for a qualified disabled individual. In that case, you may qualify for the Saver's Credit in addition to the regular benefits of the account. Contributions to ABLE accounts are not tax-deductible federally, but they can count toward the Saver's Credit for eligible low- to moderate-income taxpayers. The maximum credit is $1,000 for single filers or $2,000 for joint filers, depending on income and filing status. This credit can help families supporting individuals with disabilities grow their savings while lowering their tax bill.

Health and Insurance Credits

Premium Tax Credit (PTC)

The Premium Tax Credit (PTC) helps eligible individuals and families afford health insurance purchased through the Health Insurance Marketplace. The credit is based on your household income and the cost of benchmark plans in your area. It can be applied in advance to lower your monthly premium or claimed when you file your tax return. To qualify, your income must generally fall between 100% and 400% of the federal poverty level, though some exceptions apply. The credit amount adjusts throughout the year based on your actual income, so if you receive more in advance payments than you're eligible for, you may have to repay the excess at tax time. On the other hand, if your income is lower than expected, you may be eligible for additional credit when you file. The PTC ensures that eligible W-2 earners without employer-provided health coverage can access affordable insurance while receiving meaningful tax relief.

Other Valuable Credits:

Adoption Credit

The Adoption Credit offers financial assistance to W-2 earners who adopt a child, enabling them to claim a nonrefundable tax credit for qualified adoption expenses. For the 2025 tax year, the maximum credit is $16,810 per child, adjusted annually for inflation. Qualified expenses include adoption fees, court costs, attorney fees, and travel expenses related to the adoption process. The credit begins to phase out for taxpayers with modified adjusted gross income over $239,230 and is completely phased out at $279,230. Because it is nonrefundable, the credit can reduce your tax liability to zero, but it cannot result in a refund. However, unused amounts can be carried forward for up to five years. This credit can provide significant tax savings for families going through the adoption process and help offset the high costs associated with bringing a child into a permanent home.

Credit for the Elderly or Disabled

The Credit for the Elderly or Disabled is designed for taxpayers age sixty-five and older or permanently disabled individuals who are retired on disability income. The maximum credit is $3,750 to $7,500, depending on your income and filing status. While income limits restrict who can claim this credit, it may offer meaningful tax relief for those who qualify.

Retirement Contributions for Military Combat Pay

Even though military combat pay is not taxable, it can still count as earned income for purposes of qualifying for the Saver's Credit. This means service members with low to moderate income can still benefit from a credit of up to $1,000 ($2,000 for joint filers) by contributing to a retirement account. This rule ensures that military families don't miss out on retirement incentives just because their income is excluded from tax.

Foreign Tax Credit

If you earned investment income from foreign sources or paid taxes to a foreign government, you may be eligible for the Foreign Tax Credit. This nonrefundable credit helps avoid double taxation and can be claimed even if you do not itemize. It's most relevant to W-2 earners with foreign dividends, interest, or mutual fund investments.

State Tax Credits

In addition to federal credits, many states offer their tax credits for families, low-income earners, renters, students, and energy-efficient upgrades. These credits vary by state and may be refundable or nonrefundable. Reviewing your state tax return can uncover valuable savings that are easy to overlook if you focus only on your federal return.

Common Mistakes and Missed Opportunities

Claiming tax credits correctly requires careful attention to eligibility rules and proper documentation. Be sure you meet all the requirements for each credit and keep records such as income statements, receipts, and proof of expenses. Many taxpayers miss out on credits because they assume they earn too much or skip filing altogether. Since eligibility can change each year due to shifts in income, marital status, or education costs, it's essential to review your situation annually. You may qualify for more than one credit in the same year, such as the Child Tax Credit and the Saver's Credit, but some combinations have limitations. Coordinating your claims and prioritizing the most beneficial credits can increase your overall tax savings. Working with a tax professional can help ensure you don't overlook opportunities and that your credits are calculated and applied correctly.

Checklist: Tax Credits You Might Be Missing

- Child Tax Credit (CTC) (refundable/nonrefundable) – Do you have a qualifying child under age seventeen?
- Additional Child Tax Credit (ACTC) (refundable) – Do you qualify for a refundable portion of the CTC?
- Earned Income Tax Credit (EITC) (refundable) – Is your earned income below the threshold?
- American Opportunity Tax Credit (AOTC) (refundable/nonrefundable) – Are you or your dependent enrolled at least half-time?
- Lifetime Learning Credit (LLC) (nonrefundable) – Are you taking continuing education or job-related coursework?
- Saver's Credit (nonrefundable) – Are you contributing to a retirement account and meeting income requirements?
- Premium Tax Credit (PTC) (refundable) – Did you purchase health insurance through the Marketplace?
- Adoption Credit (nonrefundable, carryforward) – Did you adopt a child this year?
- Credit for Other Dependents (nonrefundable) – Are you supporting older children, parents, or other qualifying individuals?
- Child and Dependent Care Credit (nonrefundable) – Did you pay for child or dependent care so you could work?
- Credit for the Elderly or Disabled (nonrefundable) – Are you over 65 or permanently disabled with qualifying income?
- Military Combat Pay Saver's Credit (nonrefundable) – Did you serve in combat and contribute to retirement savings?
- Foreign Tax Credit (nonrefundable) – Did you earn foreign investment income or pay foreign taxes?

- State Tax Credits (varies) – Have you reviewed your state return for credits you may qualify for?

Final Thoughts

Tax credits can make a big difference in lowering your tax bill or increasing your refund, especially when you take the time to understand which ones apply to your situation. The credits in this chapter cover many of the most valuable opportunities available to W-2 earners, but they're not the only ones. Your eligibility can change based on income, life events, or updates to the tax law. Which is why it's always a good idea to review your options each year and speak with a qualified tax advisor to be sure you're not leaving money on the table.

Chapter Five

Tax Strategies for Single Filers – Make Your Filing Status Work for You

For many taxpayers, Single is the default filing status. It applies if you are unmarried or legally separated as of December 31st of the tax year and do not qualify for another status, such as Head of Household. Although Single filers do not get the highest standard deduction or the widest tax brackets, they still have plenty of opportunities to reduce their tax bill with smart planning.

Whether you are just starting your career, freelancing on the side, or balancing student loan payments with retirement goals, your filing status shapes your entire tax strategy. Knowing how to make the most of it can result in thousands of dollars in annual savings.

Tax Bracket Overview for Single Filers

In 2025, Single filers fall into marginal tax brackets ranging from 10% to 37%. For example, income between $48,475 and $103,350 is taxed at a rate of 22%. Understanding where your income falls in the bracket structure helps with decisions such as when to make deductible contributions, harvest capital gains, or convert traditional retirement accounts to Roth IRAs.

Example: Kaiden is single and has $75,000 in taxable income in 2025, which places him in the 22% federal tax bracket. He's considering converting $5,000 from his Traditional IRA to a Roth IRA. Because Roth conversions are treated as taxable income, the

$5,000 would be added to his existing taxable income, bringing his total to $80,000.

Since Kaiden's total income after the conversion is still within that bracket, the full $5,000 will be taxed at 22%. He would owe an additional $1,100 in federal taxes as a result of the conversion, but none of the income would be pushed into the higher 24% bracket.

By staying within his current tax bracket, Kaiden can complete the conversion without triggering a higher marginal tax rate.

Standard Deduction for Single Filers

For 2025, the standard deduction for Single filers is $15,750. That means your first $15,750 of income is not taxed at all. Unless your itemized deductions exceed that amount, claiming the standard deduction is likely the smarter move.

Planning Tip: If you are close to that threshold, consider bunching charitable contributions or prepaying deductible expenses to make itemizing worthwhile in one year, while taking the standard deduction the next.

Maximizing Education Credits

Two credits stand out for eligible Single filers:

The American Opportunity Tax Credit (AOTC) offers up to $2,500 per student for the first four years of college. As a single filer, the credit begins phasing out at a modified adjusted gross income (MAGI) of $80,000 and becomes unavailable once your income reaches $90,000.

The Lifetime Learning Credit (LLC) provides up to $2,000 per return for post-secondary courses, certifications, or graduate programs.

Example: Miah, a Single filer earning $65,000, pays $4,000 in tuition for evening classes at a local university. She qualifies for the LLC and can claim a $2,000 credit, reducing her tax directly, not just her taxable income.

Student Loan Interest Deduction

As a single filer, you may deduct up to $2,500 in student loan interest if your modified adjusted gross income (MAGI) is below $85,000. The deduction is gradually reduced once your MAGI exceeds $85,000 and is eliminated at $100,000. This is an above-the-line deduction, meaning you don't need to itemize to claim it.

Example: Jeff makes $72,000 and pays $2,500 in student loan interest. He can deduct the full amount, which lowers his taxable income and saves him several hundred dollars on his return.

Retirement Contributions and the Saver's Credit

Tax Pro Tip: If you expect to stay in the same or a higher bracket later, consider contributing to a Roth IRA now. Future withdrawals can be tax-free.

Saving for retirement comes with significant tax advantages, whether you contribute to a Traditional IRA or 401(k) (pre-tax) or a Roth IRA or Roth 401(k) (after-tax). Traditional contributions reduce your taxable income up front, lowering your tax bill for the year. Roth contributions don't give you a deduction now, but the money grows tax-free, and withdrawals in retirement are also tax-free. A single filer can contribute up to $23,500 to a 401(k) or Roth 401(k), and up to $7,000 to a Traditional or Roth IRA (plus an extra $1,000 if you're age fifty or older). However, income limits apply to Roth IRA contributions. In addition to the tax deduction or future tax-free growth, you might also qualify for the Saver's Credit, a dollar-for-dollar tax credit for low- and moderate-income earners who contribute to retirement accounts. Single filers with income below the income requirement can claim a credit worth 10%, 20%, or 50% of their retirement contributions, up to a maximum credit of $1,000.

Example: Emily earns $32,000 and contributes $2,000 to her Traditional IRA. That reduces her taxable income, and she also qualifies for a 20% Saver's Credit, giving her a $400 credit on top of the deduction. If she had contributed to a Roth IRA instead, she wouldn't receive the deduction, but she'd still qualify for the same $400 Saver's Credit.

To qualify for the credit, you must be at least eighteen, not a full-time student, and not claimed as someone else's dependent. The credit is nonrefundable, so it can bring your tax bill down to zero but won't increase your refund beyond what you've already paid.

Health Savings Account (HSA) Contributions

If you're enrolled in a high-deductible health plan (HDHP), you can contribute up to $4,150 to an HSA in 2025 as a single filer. Contributions are tax-deductible, the account grows tax-free, and qualified withdrawals for medical expenses are also tax-free. HSAs can also serve as long-term savings tools, primarily if you invest the balance and avoid dipping into it for current expenses.

Example: Ben, a healthy thirty-year-old, contributes $4,000 annually to his HSA. He pays out-of-pocket for minor medical expenses and treats the HSA like a stealth retirement account, letting the funds grow tax-free for future healthcare costs.

The downside: You must be enrolled in an HDHP to contribute, which means higher deductibles and potentially more out-of-pocket costs upfront. Also, if you use HSA funds for non-medical expenses before age sixty-five, you'll owe income tax plus a 20% penalty.

Flexible Spending Accounts (FSAs)

In 2025, you can contribute up to $3,200 of your salary to a healthcare FSA before taxes. These funds can be used for qualified expenses, such as copays, prescriptions, dental care, and vision needs. You save on both income and payroll taxes, which can cut the actual cost of your healthcare spending.

Example: Laurie expects $2,500 in orthodontic costs this year. By using an FSA, she pays for those expenses with pre-tax dollars, avoiding both federal income tax and FICA on that amount.

The downside: FSAs are typically "use it or lose it" accounts. If you don't spend the full balance by year-end (or within a short grace period, if allowed by your employer), you forfeit the leftover money. Additionally, FSAs typically don't allow investment growth or rollover, unlike HSAs.

Capital Gains and Tax-Loss Harvesting

If you hold investments for more than one year, your gains qualify for long-term capital gains tax rates, which are generally lower than ordinary income tax rates. In 2025, if your taxable income is under $47,025 (Single), your long-term capital gains are taxed at 0%. Even if you exceed those limits, you can reduce your taxable gains through tax-loss harvesting, which involves selling losing investments to offset gains.

Example: Maeva is single and sells Stock A at a $5,000 profit and Stock B at a $3,000 loss. By harvesting the loss, she only pays tax on the $2,000 net gain. If her total taxable income stays below the 0% threshold, she owes nothing in capital gains tax.

The downside: You must be careful not to trigger a wash sale, which happens if you repurchase the same or a substantially identical stock within thirty days. If you do, the IRS disallows the loss. Additionally, selling investments solely for tax reasons can disrupt your long-term investment strategy. And if your income is high, you may face the 3.8% Net Investment Income Tax (NIIT) on top of your capital gains rate.

Charitable Contributions for Itemizers

If you itemize deductions, you can deduct cash contributions up to 60% of your AGI. Donating appreciated stock lets you avoid capital gains tax and still get the full deduction based on fair market value. However, if you don't itemize, you can deduct up to $1,000 from your taxable income.

Advanced Tip: Grouping several years of donations into a single tax year can result in a significantly higher deduction, making itemizing worthwhile.

Side Hustles and Self-Employment Deductions

Single filers with side gigs must report all income over $400 and file Schedule C. You can deduct business expenses such as home office use, supplies and equipment, business miles driven, and Internet or phone usage. You may also be eligible to open a SEP IRA or a Solo 401(k), which allows higher contribution limits than a regular IRA.

Example: Marcus drives for a rideshare company part-time. He earns $10,000 and tracks $3,500 in vehicle-related expenses. After deductions, he reports a profit of $6,500 and contributes $1,000 to a SEP IRA.

New Opportunities for 2025

Thanks to the One Big Beautiful Bill Act, single filers can take advantage of several temporary but valuable tax breaks starting in 2025. Here are the key provisions:

Tax-Free Tips Deduction (Up to $25,000)

Tips earned from work are exempt from federal income tax, up to $25,000 per year, for tax years 2025 through 2028. This is especially helpful for service workers such as bartenders, delivery drivers, and hairstylists, allowing them to keep more of what they earn. The deduction reduces both taxable income and adjusted gross income (AGI), but Social Security and Medicare taxes still apply.

Overtime Deduction (Up to $12,500)

You can deduct up to $12,500 of qualified overtime wages from your taxable income for tax years 2025 through 2028. This deduction phases out when your modified adjusted gross income (MAGI) exceeds $150,000.

Expanded SALT Deduction Cap ($40,000)

The SALT deduction cap has increased to $40,000 for single filers, up from the previous $10,000 limit. The cap begins to phase out once MAGI exceeds $500,000, with the reduction being 30% of the excess income; however, it cannot fall below the minimum of $10,000. This expanded cap is in place through 2029 and will revert to $10,000 starting in tax year 2030. This change gives more single filers in high-tax states a reason to consider itemizing instead of taking the standard deduction.

Car Loan Interest Deduction (Up to $10,000)

Interest on new personal-use car loans is now deductible, up to $10,000, for vehicles purchased between 2025 and 2028. To qualify, the car must be brand new, assembled in the United States, and financed with a first-lien secured loan. The vehicle also must be used strictly for personal purposes and not for business activities.

<u>Senior Deduction ($6,000)</u>

Taxpayers age sixty-five or older may claim an additional $6,000 deduction if their MAGI is under $75,000 (single/HOH) or $12,000 if both spouses qualify and their MAGI is under $150,000 (MFJ). The deduction is available through tax year 2029 and phases out gradually at higher income levels.

Avoiding Common Tax Mistakes

- Forgetting to report freelance or 1099 income
- Claiming the AOTC when you have already used it for four years
- Deducting unqualified medical or education expenses
- Failing to update your W-4 after a raise or a new job
- Overlooking the student loan interest deduction

A little organization and awareness can prevent costly errors or missed opportunities.

Tax Strategy Checklist for Single Filers (2025)

Use this checklist to stay organized and make the most of your tax-saving opportunities as a Single filer. Review these items before you file to ensure you're taking advantage of all available deductions, credits, and planning strategies.

- Confirm Single filing status as of December 31, 2025.
- Review your tax bracket and taxable income range.
- Compare itemized deductions to the $15,750 standard deduction.
- Track qualifying education expenses for the American Opportunity or Lifetime Learning Credit.
- Calculate and claim the student loan interest deduction (if MAGI under $90,000).

- Contribute to a Traditional IRA or 401(k) to reduce taxable income.

- Check eligibility for the Saver's Credit (income under $36,500).

- Maximize HSA contributions if enrolled in a high-deductible health plan (limit: $4,150).

- Harvest capital losses to offset gains; review capital gains tax rates if income is under $47,025.

- Consider bunching charitable contributions to exceed the standard deduction threshold.

- Contribute to an FSA for expected out-of-pocket medical expenses (limit: $3,200).

- For side income, file Schedule C and track all business-related expenses.

- Open and contribute to a SEP IRA or Solo 401(k) if self-employed.

- Use the IRS Withholding Estimator to check if your W-4 needs to be adjusted.

- Avoid common mistakes: unreported income, ineligible credits, or missing documentation.

- Consult a tax professional if your situation includes investments, freelance work, or education-related claims.

Final Thoughts on Single Filer Tax Strategy

Being a Single filer does not mean you have fewer opportunities. The flexibility and simplicity of this status can be an advantage if you know where to look. With smart use of credits, contributions, and deductions, you can reduce your tax burden significantly. Think ahead, keep good records, and revisit your plan as life changes. Tax time should be about what you own, not just what you owe.

Chapter Six

Tax Strategies for Married Filing Jointly – The Power of Filing Together

Married Filing Jointly (MFJ) is the most commonly used and most advantageous filing status for married couples. It allows both spouses to combine their incomes and deductions on a single tax return, and in most cases, this results in a lower total tax bill. The IRS rewards joint filers with wider tax brackets, higher standard deductions, and access to valuable tax credits that are often limited or unavailable to those who file separately.

Whether both spouses are working full-time, one earns more than the other, or one is staying home with the kids, understanding how to optimize the MFJ status can unlock substantial savings.

Tax Bracket Advantages for MFJ Filers

The most immediate benefit of filing jointly is access to broader income thresholds within each tax bracket. In 2025, the 22% bracket extends up to $206,700 for married filing jointly (MFJ) filers. By comparison, the same bracket for single filers ends at just $103,350. This means more of your income is taxed at lower rates when you file together.

Example: Mike earns $150,000, and his wife, Jeny, earns $40,000. If they filed separately, Mike's income would push more of his wages into the 24% bracket. By filing jointly, their combined $190,000 falls within the 22% bracket, lowering their effective tax rate.

This structure is especially valuable for couples with uneven incomes, since it allows the higher-earning spouse to benefit from the lower-earning spouse's unused bracket space.

Standard Deduction, Itemizing, and Other MFJ Benefits

Married Filing Jointly filers receive a standard deduction of $31,500 in 2025, which automatically lowers taxable income without the need to track every deductible expense. For many families, this is the more straightforward and more beneficial option. However, if your itemized deductions, such as mortgage interest, property taxes, charitable contributions, and out-of-pocket medical costs, add up to more than the standard deduction, itemizing could result in a lower tax bill. It is worth comparing both options annually to determine which one provides the greater benefit. Additionally, joint filers are eligible for most major tax credits, including the Earned Income Tax Credit, Child Tax Credit, American Opportunity and Lifetime Learning Credits, the Saver's Credit, and the Dependent Care Credit.

Many of these credits are either reduced or entirely disallowed if you file separately, which is why most couples benefit from filing jointly whenever possible.

Combining Incomes Strategically

When one spouse earns significantly more than the other, MFJ status provides a powerful income-smoothing effect. It allows income to be averaged across the couple, helping avoid higher marginal tax rates.

Example: A household where one spouse earns $200,000 and the other earns $50,000 might worry that the high-income spouse will face steep tax rates. However, filing jointly allows their combined $250,000 income to be taxed progressively, with a large portion falling into the lower 10%, 12%, and 22% tax brackets.

This is one of the simplest yet most impactful benefits of filing jointly.

New: Deduct Up to $25,000 in Qualified Overtime Pay

Starting in 2025, taxpayers may deduct up to $12,500 of qualified overtime pay per filer, with a maximum of $25,000 for married couples filing jointly. This deduction applies to W-2 employees whose overtime wages meet the IRS definition of "qualified overtime," which generally refers to hours worked beyond 40 per week and paid at a rate of at least one and a half times the regular rate of pay.

Overtime often pushes workers into higher tax brackets or increases their Adjusted Gross Income (AGI), which can reduce eligibility for credits such as the Child Tax Credit or Saver's Credit. By allowing filers to deduct this income, the One Big Beautiful Bill Act lowers taxable income even if you don't itemize, reduces AGI, and helps preserve eligibility for phaseout-sensitive tax benefits.

Example: Maria and Kevin are married and file jointly. Kevin earns a base salary of $60,000 and makes $15,000 in qualified overtime pay. Maria earns $40,000. Under the new law, Kevin can deduct $12,500 of his overtime pay, reducing their joint taxable income. This lowers their tax bill by several thousand dollars, depending on their marginal tax rate and the credits they qualify for.

Retirement Contributions: Doubling the Benefits

Married couples can each contribute to retirement accounts, effectively doubling their household's annual savings limits. In 2025, anyone under age fifty can contribute up to $23,500 to a 401(k), 403(b), 457(b), or Thrift Savings Plan. Those aged fifty or older can contribute up to $31,000 thanks to a $7,500 catch-up allowance. Under SECURE 2.0, those aged sixty to sixty-three may qualify for an even higher 401(k) catch-up limit of $11,250 if their plan allows it.

For IRAs, the contribution limit remains $7,000. Individuals aged fifty or older can contribute an additional $1,000, bringing the total contribution to $8,000.

Example: Lisa and Patrick, both fifty-two years old, contribute $31,000 each to their 401(k) plans and $8,000 each to their IRAs. Together, they set aside $78,000 in tax-advantaged savings for the year. Depending on the type of account and their income, these contributions may be deductible or grow tax-free.

Quick Math Example: If both spouses max out their 401(k) contributions at $23,500 each, that's $47,000 deducted from taxable income before employer contributions are even added.

Income Phase-Out Rules

Deductibility and eligibility for IRAs and Roth IRAs depend on income and filing status:

- Traditional IRA Deduction Phase-Out (if covered by a workplace plan):
- Married filing jointly (contributing spouse covered): $126,000 to $146,000
- Married filing jointly (contributing spouse not covered but spouse is): $236,000 to $246,000

Roth IRA Contribution Phase-Out:

- Married filing jointly: $236,000 to $246,000

If you're married and a workplace plan covers neither spouse, the traditional IRA deduction is not subject to any income limits.

Health Savings Accounts (HSAs)

Families enrolled in a high-deductible health plan (HDHP) can contribute up to $8,550 in 2025 to a family HSA. These contributions are tax-deductible, grow tax-free, and can be withdrawn tax-free for qualified medical expenses. If either spouse is fifty-five or older, they can contribute an additional $1,000 catch-up contribution.

Tip: HSAs are one of the few accounts that offer triple tax advantages: deductible contributions, tax-free growth, and tax-free distributions. They are an excellent long-term tool for both health and retirement planning.

Claiming Children and Dependents

If a married couple filing jointly has qualifying children or dependents, they may be eligible for several valuable tax credits. The Child Tax Credit provides up to $2,200 per qualifying child, with up to $1,700 of the credit being refundable if the amount exceeds the taxpayer's tax liability. They may also claim the Child and Dependent Care Credit, which allows a percentage of up to $6,000 in qualifying childcare expenses for two or more children. Depending on income, the maximum savings are $2,100. Additionally, if they have children or dependents in college, they may be eligible for education credits, such as the American Opportunity Tax Credit or the Lifetime Learning Credit.

Example: Ben and Anna, married filing jointly, have two young children and pay $7,000 in daycare expenses. They qualify for a $1,400 Dependent Care Credit (20% of $7,000, since their income exceeds $43,000) and also receive $4,400 in Child Tax Credits for their two children. Together, these credits reduce their overall tax liability by $5,800.

Dependent Care Flexible Spending Account (DCAP)

Married couples filing jointly can also benefit from a Dependent Care Flexible Spending Account (DCAP), if offered by one spouse's employer. This account allows you to set aside up to $5,000 per household in pre-tax dollars to cover childcare or dependent care expenses, including daycare, preschool, before- and after-school programs, or in-home care for a dependent adult. These contributions lower your taxable income, providing upfront tax savings that often exceed the value of the Child and Dependent Care Credit for higher-earning couples. Because the DCAP and the tax credit can't be used on the same expenses, it's worth comparing both options to see which saves more. For many dual-income households, using a DCAP is one of the most efficient ways to reduce their tax bill while covering a real-life expense.

Example: Carlos and Maya are married, filing jointly, and both work full-time. Their combined income is $110,000. They have two children in daycare and pay $10,000 per year for care, allowing them to work.

Option 1: Use a Dependent Care FSA (DCAP)

Carlos's employer offers a Dependent Care FSA. He contributes the maximum allowed, $5,000, to the account through payroll deductions.

Because the $5,000 is pre-tax, they save on:

- Federal income tax (22% bracket): $5,000 × 22% = $1,100
- Social Security tax (6.2%): $5,000 × 6.2% = $310
- Medicare tax (1.45%): $5,000 × 1.45% = $72.50
- Total tax savings = $1,482.50

Option 2: Claim the Child and Dependent Care Credit

Instead of using the FSA, Carlos and Maya pay the full $10,000 out of pocket and claim the Child and Dependent Care Credit on their tax return. For income over $43,000, the credit rate is 20%.

They can use up to $6,000 of qualifying expenses for two children.

Tax credit = $6,000 × 20% = $1,200

In this case, the Dependent Care FSA provides greater tax savings. However, if their income were much lower, the percentage used to calculate the tax credit would be higher (up to 35%), which could make the credit more valuable than the FSA.

Capital Gains and Investment Income

Couples filing jointly can realize long-term capital gains tax-free if their taxable income is under $94,050 in 2025. If income exceeds that, gains are taxed at 15% or 20%, depending on the amount.

Example: Alix and Mirlene sell long-term investments with a $10,000 gain. Their total income is $85,000, so the capital gains fall under the 0% threshold. They pay no federal tax on the gain.

MFJ status offers opportunities for tax-efficient investing, particularly for couples managing capital assets.

Charitable Contributions Planning

MFJ filers can deduct cash donations up to 60% of their adjusted gross income (AGI) when they itemize. If you are looking to make a significant gift, consider using a Donor-Advised Fund (DAF) to donate a lump sum now and distribute funds to charities over time.

Tip: Donating appreciated stock not only qualifies for a deduction at fair market value but also helps avoid capital gains tax on the appreciation.

Spousal IRA Contributions

Even if one spouse isn't working, the couple can still contribute to an IRA on their behalf. The working spouse may contribute up to $7,000 (or $8,000 if the nonworking spouse is age fifty or older) to a Spousal IRA, providing a valuable tax-advantaged opportunity.

Example: Kim works full-time, while her husband, Tom, stays home with their children. Kim earns enough to support contributions to both of their IRAs, helping them save more for retirement while reducing their taxable income for the current year.

Education Credits and Deductions

Married couples with a MAGI under $180,000 can qualify for:

- The American Opportunity Tax Credit: up to $2,500 per eligible student
- The Lifetime Learning Credit: up to $2,000 per return

Example: Both parents are taking night classes to advance their careers. If they spend $6,000 in tuition and fees, they may be eligible for both education credits, depending on eligibility and timing.

Avoiding the Marriage Penalty

While most couples benefit from filing jointly, high-income earners may occasionally face the so-called marriage penalty, when combining incomes causes them to lose deductions or credits.

One example is the Medicare surtax, which applies to earnings above $250,000 for married filing jointly (MFJ), compared to $200,000 for single filers. That threshold is not doubled, which can result in unexpected taxes for dual high-income households.

To mitigate this, consider deferring income to a future year, bunching deductions, and make sure to review your filing options each year, especially if your income fluctuates.

Filing Jointly vs. Separately: When Not to File Jointly

Although MFJ is usually best, consider Married Filing Separately (MFS) in cases such as one spouse has significant medical expenses, which are only deductible above 7.5% of AGI, one spouse has past legal liabilities or delinquent taxes, or there are legal reasons to keep finances separate.

Please note that most credits are reduced or disallowed under MFS; therefore, be sure to compare them carefully before choosing this path.

New Opportunities for 2025 (Married Filing Jointly)

Beginning in 2025, married couples filing jointly will benefit from a set of temporary tax breaks introduced under the Tax One Big Beautiful Bill Act. Below are the main highlights:

Tax-Free Tips Deduction (Up to $25,000)

Married couples can each exclude up to $12,500 in tip income from federal income tax for tax years 2025 through 2028. The deduction reduces both taxable income and adjusted gross income (AGI). Social Security and Medicare taxes still apply. This is especially beneficial for households where one or both spouses earn tips, such as in hospitality or delivery services.

Overtime Deduction (Up to $12,500)

Joint filers can deduct up to $12,500 of qualified overtime wages from taxable income for 2025 through 2028. This deduction begins to phase out when your combined MAGI exceeds $300,000.

Expanded SALT Deduction Cap ($40,000)

The State and Local Tax (SALT) deduction cap increases to $40,000 (up from $10,000) for married couples filing jointly. The cap for this filing status begins to phase out once MAGI exceeds $500,000. This expanded cap will increase by 1% and it is effective through 2029; after that, the original $10,000 cap will be reinstated in 2030.

Watch Out: The expanded SALT deduction still carries a marriage penalty. A couple may hit the phaseout sooner together than they would as single filers.

Car Loan Interest Deduction (Up to $10,000)

Interest on new personal-use car loans is now deductible, up to $10,000, for vehicles purchased between 2025 and 2028. To qualify, the car must be brand new, assembled in the United States, and financed with a first-lien secured loan. The vehicle also must be used strictly for personal purposes and not for business activities.

Senior Deduction ($6,000)

If one or both spouses are age 65 or older and the couple's MAGI is below $150,000, they may claim an additional deduction of $6,000 per qualifying taxpayer, up to $12,000 if both spouses qualify, through tax year 2029. Specific eligibility criteria apply.

Tax Strategy Checklist for Married Filing Jointly (2025)

Use this checklist to guide your tax planning and maximize savings as a Married Filing Jointly (MFJ) couple. Review these items before filing your return or making year-end decisions.

- Confirm MFJ filing status eligibility as of December 31st, 2025.
- Review income levels and take advantage of wider MFJ tax brackets.
- Use the $31,500 standard deduction if itemizing is not beneficial.
- Estimate eligibility for the Child Tax Credit, Earned Income Credit, and Dependent Care Credit.
- Contribute to both spouses' 401(k) plans (up to $23,500 each, or $31,000 if age 50+).
- Maximize HSA contributions (up to $8,300 for families, plus $1,000 catch-up per spouse age 55+).
- Claim the American Opportunity or Lifetime Learning Credit (MAGI under $180,000).

- Consider spousal IRA contributions for a non-working or low-income spouse.

- Harvest capital losses or plan investment sales based on the $94,050 0% capital gains threshold.

- Plan charitable giving (up to 60% of AGI deductible); consider using a Donor-Advised Fund.

- Evaluate if bunching deductions makes itemizing more beneficial this year.

- Consider MFS only if facing significant medical expenses, legal issues, or other exceptional circumstances.

- Keep records of tuition, fees, and expenses for education credits.

- Organize receipts and documentation for any itemized deductions if not taking the standard deduction.

- Consult with a CPA or tax professional if income exceeds credit limits or if your return includes business, rental, or investment income.

Final Thoughts on MFJ Strategies

Filing jointly is more than just checking a box on your tax return; it is a powerful tool that can lower your tax bill, boost your retirement savings, and support your long-term financial goals. The key is to plan early and revisit your strategies each year, especially as your family, income, or expenses change.

Whether you are navigating a dual-income household or balancing a one-income family, the Married Filing Jointly status offers flexibility, savings, and access to tax benefits that are hard to beat. When used strategically, it can put you and your spouse on a more secure financial path.

Chapter Seven

Tax Strategies for Married Filing Separately – When Splitting Returns Can Save or Shield

Married Filing Separately (MFS) is one of the five federal filing statuses, but it is often misunderstood or overlooked. In most cases, it results in higher taxes, limited access to credits, and reduced eligibility for deductions. However, in the right situation, MFS is not only practical but also strategic.

Think of MFS as a tool for financial clarity, protection, and separation. It is not the default choice, but in marriages facing legal issues, debt concerns, or significant medical costs, it can be the smarter path.

When Filing Separately Is a Strategic Move

Most couples benefit from filing jointly, but MFS becomes appealing when one spouse faces significant medical expenses, past-due tax or loan obligations, a pending divorce, or legal or financial risk.

Example: Joseph and Paula are married. Joseph owes back taxes and is subject to IRS garnishment. If they file jointly, their refund could be seized to pay Joseph's debt. Filing separately allows Paula to protect her refund and remain compliant.

Married Filing Separately can also be beneficial for couples who wish to keep their finances private or who reside in separate states and are required to file separately due to local regulations.

Medical Expense Deduction Strategy

Medical expenses are only deductible once they exceed 7.5% of your adjusted gross income (AGI). Filing separately can lower the AGI threshold if one spouse earns much less.

Example: Samantha and Ashley have $10,000 in unreimbursed medical bills. If they file jointly and their adjusted gross income (AGI) is $120,000, only expenses exceeding $9,000 would be deductible. However, if Ashley earns just $40,000 and they file separately, the deductible amount starts after $3,000, making a larger portion of their expenses count toward the deductible.

This can be a key strategy for couples dealing with chronic illness, long-term care, or high out-of-pocket health costs.

Avoiding Joint Liability for Tax Debts

This is one of the biggest reasons to file separately. When you file jointly, both spouses are jointly and severally liable, meaning the IRS can hold either of you responsible for the entire tax bill, even if one spouse underreports income or claims inappropriate deductions.

Example: Mark is self-employed and had a bad year, including underreporting some income. His wife, Minerve, works full-time with consistent W-2 income. By filing separately, Minerve avoids being responsible for errors on Mark's return.

For couples who do not fully trust each other's bookkeeping or want to protect themselves during times of financial uncertainty, MFS is a safeguard.

Asset Protection and Legal Separation

In divorce or separation situations, emotions and finances can get tangled. Filing separately helps maintain clear records and boundaries during these transitions.

Example: Brittany and Thomas are separated and heading toward divorce. Brittany wants to protect her return from any claims Thomas might make about shared assets or deductions. Filing separately ensures that each person reports only their income and deductions.

In some cases, attorneys even recommend MFS to support legal boundaries between spouses while proceedings are underway.

Handling Itemized Deductions on Separate Returns

This is where coordination becomes essential. If one spouse itemizes, the other must itemize too, even if they would benefit more from taking the standard deduction.

Strategy: Decide who will benefit more from claiming shared deductions, such as mortgage interest or property taxes. That spouse can itemize, and the other can match, even if they don't have many deductions.

Example: Mia and Daniel own a home together. Daniel paid all $10,000 of the mortgage interest. They agree that Daniel should itemize, and Mia must itemize too, even though she only has $2,000 in deductions.

Student Loan and Education Deductions

Married Filing Separately (MFS) filers cannot claim the student loan interest deduction and are not eligible for the American Opportunity or Lifetime Learning Tax Credits. That sounds like a deal-breaker, but sometimes it isn't.

Example: If one spouse has no qualifying education expenses or their income is too high to benefit from the credit anyway, then not being eligible for those credits under MFS is a non-issue. In short, if you are not losing a benefit, there is nothing lost.

Impact on Retirement Account Contributions

This is one of the downsides of MFS. For 2025, the phase-out range for deducting contributions to a traditional IRA starts at $0 and ends at $10,000 if a workplace retirement plan covers either spouse. Similarly, Roth IRA contributions phase out completely once the modified adjusted gross income (MAGI) reaches $10,000 for married filing separately (MFS) filers. That means IRA planning under MFS is severely limited. You may still contribute, but the deduction or eligibility might be reduced or eliminated.

Watch Out: IRA deductions phase out at just $10,000 of income if a retirement plan covers your spouse. That limit makes it nearly impossible for most MFS filers to deduct IRA contributions.

State Tax Strategy Considerations

In community property states, such as California, Texas, or Arizona, filing separately can become complicated. Income and deductions may have to be split 50/50, even if one spouse earned all the income.

Example: In California, Maria earns $100,000, and her spouse earns nothing. Under community property rules, each spouse would report $50,000 of income. If they file separately without coordinating, they risk mismatches that could trigger audits or delays.

For couples in these states, filing jointly is usually easier; however, married filing separately (MFS) is still possible if well-planned.

Coordination Is Key with MFS; both spouses file their returns, but the IRS still expects consistency between them. That includes not double-claiming dependents, reporting shared income or deductions consistently, and agreeing on who will claim which credits and or deductions.

Note that there are significant Tax Credit Limitations Under MFS. MFS filers generally cannot claim the Earned Income Tax Credit, education credits, and the Dependent Care Credit. They are also more likely to face reduced deduction thresholds, as seen with IRA contributions and phaseouts. These trade-offs should not be ignored. Run the numbers before making a decision.

Potential for Filing Jointly Later

There is good news. If you file separately and later change your mind, you can amend your return and switch to Married Filing Jointly within three years of the original due date.

Example: Rachel and James filed separately during a contentious year. Two years later, they have reconciled and realize they could have saved thousands by filing jointly. They file Form 1040-X and amend both returns to be married filing jointly (MFJ).

This flexibility allows couples time to reevaluate their situation if circumstances improve.

Married Filing Separately Often Means Paying More

Filing as Married Filing Separately (MFS) generally results in a higher tax bill and fewer benefits. Many valuable credits and deductions are off-limits or significantly reduced for MFS filers. These include the Earned Income Tax Credit, the Child and Dependent Care Credit, education credits (like the American Opportunity and Lifetime Learning Credits), and the deduction for student loan interest. MFS filers also face a lower income phaseout for deductible IRA contributions and must both itemize if one spouse does, even if the other has no deductions. The Tax One Big Beautiful Bill Act introduced additional benefits that are only available to joint filers: MFS taxpayers are not eligible for the Tax-Free Tips exclusion (up to $25,000) or the Overtime Pay Deduction (up to $12,500). These new deductions can provide real relief for working families, but they're off the table if you file separately. Unless there are legal or financial reasons to keep your tax life separate, filing jointly usually results in a much better outcome.

Tax Strategy Checklist for Married Filing Separately (2025)

Use this checklist to evaluate whether Married Filing Separately (MFS) is the right option for you and to guide your planning. This filing status is not always optimal, but it can offer significant benefits under certain circumstances.

- Confirm MFS status is appropriate based on your marital and legal situation as of December 31st, 2025.

- Determine if one spouse has significant medical expenses that exceed 7.5% of their AGI.

- Consider filing separately if one spouse owes back taxes, child support, or student loan debt.

- Understand that MFS filers are not eligible for the Earned Income Credit, education credits, or the Dependent Care Credit.

- Evaluate retirement plan limits, deductions for Traditional and Roth IRAs, and phase out quickly under MFS.

- If one spouse itemizes deductions, ensure both spouses itemize and coordinate deductions accurately.

- In community property states, divide income and deductions 50/50 unless exceptions apply.

- Ensure consistent reporting between both returns, including dependents, mortgage interest, and other shared items, to match.

- Use MFS to protect your refund if your spouse is subject to IRS garnishment or legal claims.

- Keep documentation for all medical, legal, or asset-related reasons for choosing MFS.

- Consider using MFS during divorce or legal separation for financial clarity.

- Revisit your choice annually and consider amending to MFJ within 3 years if circumstances improve.

- Work with a CPA or tax advisor to calculate both MFJ and MFS outcomes before filing.

- Keep all related correspondence and IRS publications (502, 970, 590-A, and 555) for reference.

- Review state tax rules that may affect how MFS is treated in your state.

Final Thoughts on MFS Tax Strategy

Married Filing Separately is not the most common or tax-friendly filing status, but under the right circumstances, it can become a smart option. It can help reduce liability exposure, protect refunds, simplify legal transitions, and provide clarity in complex financial arrangements.

If you are considering MFS, talk to a CPA or tax advisor before filing. This status comes with strict rules and narrow margins, but with proper coordination, it can serve as an effective part of your financial and legal planning.

Chapter Eight

Tax Strategies for Head of Household Filers – The Advantage of Going Solo, Strategically

Head of Household (HOH) is one of the most valuable filing statuses for single individuals with dependents. It provides a higher standard deduction and wider tax brackets than the Single status, helping to reduce tax liability. Yet not everyone who qualifies takes full advantage, and some mistakenly claim the status without meeting the criteria. Understanding the rules and opportunities that come with HOH can save you thousands.

Eligibility Requirements

To qualify for HOH, you must be unmarried or considered unmarried as of December 31st, pay more than half the cost of maintaining your household, and have a qualifying person, such as a child or dependent relative, living with you for more than half the year. For example, if you are divorced, earn $60,000, and your child lives with you the majority of the year, you likely qualify. But if the child lives with the other parent, even if you pay child support, you may not meet the requirement. Misunderstanding who qualifies as a dependent is a frequent mistake that can lead to IRS scrutiny.

Tax Bracket Benefits for HOH Filers

One of the biggest perks of HOH status is access to more favorable tax brackets. For instance, in 2025, the 12% bracket extends to $64,850 for HOH filers compared to $48,475 for Single filers. This means more of your income is taxed at lower rates, giving you extra room before hitting higher tax brackets.

Tax Pro Tip: Filing as Head of Household gives you a higher standard deduction than Single status and wider tax brackets. If you qualify, it almost always lowers your tax bill.

Standard Deduction and Itemizing

In 2025, Head of Household filers receive a standard deduction of $23,625, which is higher than the $15,750 available to single filers. This reduces your taxable income automatically without the need to itemize deductions. However, if your total itemized deductions, such as mortgage interest, state and local taxes, and charitable contributions, are more than your standard deduction, it may still be beneficial to itemize. For many single parents, the larger standard deduction offers significant savings, even on a simple tax return.

Claiming Dependents and the Child Tax Credit

Head of Household (HOH) filers may be eligible for the Child Tax Credit of up to $2,200 per Qualifying Child under age seventeen, with up to $1,700 of it refundable. To claim the credit, the child must meet specific age, relationship, residency, and support tests. In some cases, a qualifying relative may also provide tax benefits, though they do not qualify for the Child Tax Credit. For example, suppose your niece lives with you and you provide more than half of her support. In that case, she may meet the criteria as either a Qualifying Child or a Qualifying Relative, depending on her age and other factors.

Earned Income Tax Credit (EITC) for HOH Filers

The EITC is one of the most generous refundable credits available. In 2025, an HOH filer with two qualifying children earning under $55,000 could receive over $6,500. That's not a deduction, it's money in your pocket, even if you owe no taxes. However, eligibility depends on income, filing status, and number of dependents.

Education Credits and Deductions

If you're paying college expenses, the American Opportunity Tax Credit (AOTC) can provide up to $2,500 per student. The Lifetime Learning Credit offers up to $2,000 per return for graduate or continuing education. For example, a working parent paying for evening classes might qualify.

Child and Dependent Care Credit

HOH filers paying for daycare or after-school care may be eligible for the Child and Dependent Care Credit. This credit is based on a percentage of your qualifying expenses, which can be up to $3,000 for one child or $6,000 for two or more. The percentage you can claim depends on your adjusted gross income (AGI). The credit is non-refundable, which means it can lower your tax bill to zero but does not result in a refund if there's any leftover amount. Be sure to track all eligible expenses and include the provider's information when you file.

Dependent Care Flexible Spending Account (DCAP)

Single parents filing as Head of Household (HOH) can benefit from a Dependent Care Flexible Spending Account (DCAP) if their employer offers one. This account allows you to set aside up to $5,000 per year in pre-tax dollars to pay for childcare or dependent care expenses, including daycare, preschool, before- and after-school programs, summer day camps, or in-home care for a dependent adult. Because contributions are made before taxes, they reduce your taxable income and result in direct tax savings. In many cases, a DCAP offers greater savings than the Child and Dependent Care Credit, especially for higher earners. However, you can't use both benefits for the same expenses, so it's worth comparing which option gives you the bigger break. For working parents with eligible expenses, a DCAP is a practical and efficient way to lower your tax bill.

Example: Jessica is a single mother filing as Head of Household. She earns $85,000 per year and pays $9,000 annually for daycare for her two young children, allowing her to work.

Option 1: Use a Dependent Care FSA (DCAP)

Jessica's employer offers a DCAP, and she contributes the maximum $5,000 through payroll deductions.

Because these contributions are pre-tax, she saves:

Federal income tax (22% bracket): $5,000 × 22% = $1,100

Social Security tax (6.2%): $5,000 × 6.2% = $310

Medicare tax (1.45%): $5,000 × 1.45% = $72.50

Total tax savings = $1,482.50

Option 2: Claim the Child and Dependent Care Credit

If Jessica doesn't use the DCAP, she can claim the credit instead. Since her income is over $43,000, she qualifies for the minimum credit rate of 20%.

She can apply up to $6,000 of her care expenses toward the credit:

Tax credit = $6,000 × 20% = $1,200

Health Insurance Premium Tax Credit (PTC)

If you buy health insurance through the marketplace, you may qualify for the PTC. Because income limits are higher for HOH filers than for Singles, you may receive more premium assistance.

Retirement Savings Contributions Credit (Saver's Credit)

HOH filers earning under $59,250 in 2025 may qualify for the Saver's Credit, worth up to $1,000. This credit rewards you for contributing to retirement accounts, such as an IRA or 401(k).

Charitable Contributions and Deductions

If you itemize your deductions, charitable donations can reduce your taxable income. Another strategy is "bunching" multiple years of donations into one tax year to help you exceed the standard deduction. Under the new law, even if you don't itemize, you may still deduct up to $1,000 in charitable contributions. This makes it easier for more taxpayers to benefit from giving, even while taking the standard deduction.

New Opportunities for 2025 (Head of Household)

Beginning in 2025, individuals filing as Head of Household will have access to new tax breaks introduced under the Tax One Big Beautiful Bill Act. These temporary changes aim to provide extra relief for single parents and others with qualifying dependents.

Tax-Free Tips (Up to $25,000)

HOH filers can exclude up to $25,000 in tip income from federal taxation each year from 2025 through 2028. This is especially helpful for those working in service jobs who are also supporting a household.

Overtime Deduction (Up to $12,500)

If you work extra hours, you can deduct up to $12,500 of qualified overtime pay from your taxable income. This benefit phases out once your MAGI exceeds $150,000.

Expanded SALT Deduction Cap ($40,000)

The SALT deduction cap is increased to $40,000 for Head of Household filers, a substantial rise from the previous $10,000 limit. The cap for this filing status begins to phase out once MAGI exceeds $500,000. This expanded cap will increase by 1% and it is effective through 2029; after that, the original $10,000 cap will be reinstated in 2030.

Car Loan Interest Deduction (Up to $10,000)

Interest on new personal-use car loans is now deductible, up to $10,000, for vehicles purchased between 2025 and 2028. To qualify, the car must be brand new, assembled in the United States, and financed with a first-lien secured loan. The vehicle also must be used strictly for personal purposes and not for business activities.

Senior Deduction ($6,000)

If you are sixty-five or older and your MAGI is under $75,000, you may qualify for an additional $6,000 deduction. This deduction is available through tax year 2029 and requires meeting certain conditions.

These deductions can add up to meaningful savings, especially for Head of Household filers managing family expenses on a single income.

Tax Pitfalls to Avoid for HOH Filers

Common pitfalls include claiming the status without a qualifying dependent, misreporting custody arrangements, or failing to provide documentation of household expenses. Keep detailed records, including custody agreements and receipts for rent, groceries, and utilities.

Sometimes it's more beneficial for the noncustodial parent to claim the child, especially if they provide most of the financial support. The custodial parent might choose to file as Single if it results in higher total tax savings across both households.

Tax Strategy Checklist for Head of Household Filers (2025)

This checklist is designed to help Head of Household (HOH) filers ensure they are eligible for the status and maximize tax savings. Review each item to confirm you are taking advantage of all the benefits available in 2025.

- Confirm HOH eligibility: Unmarried or considered unmarried as of December 31st, with a qualifying dependent living with you more than half the year.

- Ensure you pay more than half the cost of maintaining the household (rent, mortgage, utilities, groceries).

- Use the HOH standard deduction of $23,625 if you do not itemize.

- Determine where your income falls in the HOH tax bracket to plan for withholding and credits.

- Claim the Child Tax Credit: up to $2,200 per qualifying child under age 17 (up to $1,700 refundable).

- Check eligibility for the Earned Income Tax Credit (EITC), especially if you have one or more children.

- Consider the American Opportunity Tax Credit or Lifetime Learning Credit for education expenses.

- If you pay for childcare, check eligibility for the Child and Dependent Care Credit (up to $2,100 for two children).

- Explore the Premium Tax Credit (PTC) if you buy health insurance through the marketplace.

- Contribute to a retirement plan and check eligibility for the Saver's Credit (up to $1,000 if income under $59,250).

- If itemizing, track and document charitable contributions. Consider bunching donations for higher deductions.

- Use the IRS Withholding Estimator to avoid surprises at tax time and to manage credit claims.

- Maintain documentation for child custody, household payments, and qualifying dependent criteria.

- If filing with a noncustodial co-parent, consider whether it is more beneficial for you or the other parent to claim the child for certain credits.

- Review your filing status annually and consult a tax advisor for complex situations or custody arrangements.

Final Thoughts on HOH Tax Strategies

The Head of Household status offers a blend of flexibility and valuable tax benefits for qualifying individuals. Stay organized, confirm your eligibility each year, and take advantage of every deduction and credit available to lighten your tax burden.

Chapter Nine

Tax Strategies for Qualifying Widow(er) with Dependent Child – Extending the Benefits of Joint Filing

The Qualifying Widow(er) with Dependent Child filing status allows surviving spouses with dependents to retain the same tax benefits as those who file jointly. For two years following the year of a spouse's death, this status helps families maintain financial continuity. For example, if your spouse died in 2025, you may claim Qualifying Widow(er) status in 2026 and 2027. The status is only available for two tax years after the year your spouse passed away. After that, your filing status may change to Head of Household or Single, depending on your situation.

Example: After losing her husband in 2024, Maria continued to care for their eight-year-old son. She filed her 2024 tax return as Married Filing Jointly. In 2025 and 2026, she qualifies for the Qualifying Widow(er) status because she remains unmarried, her son lives with her full-time, and she pays all the household expenses. This allows her to continue benefiting from the larger standard deduction and wider tax brackets.

Eligibility Requirements

To qualify, all of the following must be true:

- Your spouse died in the previous two tax years.
- You did not remarry before the end of the current year.

- You have a child or stepchild whom you can claim as a dependent.
- You paid more than half the cost of keeping up a home that was the primary residence of you and the child.

Tax Benefits Compared to Other Statuses: This status grants access to the same tax brackets and standard deduction as Married Filing Jointly. This can lead to substantial savings compared to filing as Single or Head of Household, especially during the early years of raising children alone.

IRS Reminder: You can use Married Filing Jointly rates for up to two years after a spouse's death if you have a dependent child, but you must file as Qualifying Widow(er).

Standard Deduction, Itemized Deduction, and Brackets

For tax year 2025, the standard deduction is $31,500, which reduces your taxable income directly. Broader tax brackets mean more of your income is taxed at lower rates, increasing your after-tax income. If your total deductible expenses, such as mortgage interest, charitable contributions, and state or local taxes, are higher than the standard deduction, itemizing may give you a greater tax benefit.

Tax Benefits for Qualifying Widowers with Dependent Children

If you're a qualifying widower with a dependent child, you may be eligible for the Child Tax Credit of up to $2,200 per qualifying child under age seventeen, with up to $1,700 refundable. To qualify, the child must meet age, relationship, residency, and support tests. In some cases, a qualifying relative, such as a niece or nephew, may still provide a tax benefit, although they do not qualify for the Child Tax Credit. Whether the child qualifies depends on their age, your relationship to them, and the level of support you provide.

Earned Income Tax Credit (EITC)

For 2025, a qualifying widower with two dependent children and earned income under $55,000 could receive more than $7,000 through the EITC. This is a refundable credit, meaning you can receive it even if you owe no tax. Eligibility is determined by income, filing status, and the number of qualifying children.

Education Credits and Deductions

If you're paying college expenses for your child or yourself, you may qualify for valuable education credits. The American Opportunity Tax Credit (AOTC) provides up to $2,500 per student for the first four years of college. The Lifetime Learning Credit offers up to $2,000 per return for graduate or continuing education. A surviving spouse returning to school while supporting children may qualify for either credit.

Child and Dependent Care Credit

If you pay for childcare so you can work or look for work, you may be eligible for the Child and Dependent Care Credit. This credit is based on a percentage of your qualifying expenses, which can be up to $3,000 for one child or $6,000 for two or more. The percentage you can claim depends on your adjusted gross income (AGI). The credit is non-refundable, which means it can lower your tax bill to zero but does not result in a refund if there's any leftover amount. Be sure to track all eligible expenses and include the provider's information when you file.

Dependent Care Flexible Spending Account (DCAP)

A Qualifying Widow(er) with a dependent child can benefit from a Dependent Care Flexible Spending Account (DCAP) if their employer offers one. This account allows up to $5,000 per year to be set aside in pre-tax dollars to pay for eligible dependent care expenses. These include daycare, preschool, before- and after-school programs, summer day camps, or care for a dependent adult. Contributions are made through payroll deductions and reduce both taxable income and payroll taxes. For many taxpayers using the Qualifying Widow(er) filing status, a DCAP can provide more savings than the Child and Dependent Care Credit. However, the same expenses cannot be used for both benefits, so it is essential to compare the options. For working parents managing care costs after the loss of a spouse, a DCAP can be a practical way to lower taxes and ease the financial burden of care.

Example: Maria is a qualifying widow with one dependent child. She earns $95,000 per year and pays $7,500 annually for childcare, allowing her to continue working full-time.

<u>Option 1: Use a Dependent Care FSA (DCAP)</u>

Maria's employer offers a DCAP. She contributes the full $5,000 through payroll deductions.

Because these dollars are not subject to tax, her savings include:

Federal income tax (22 percent bracket): $5,000 × 22% = $1,100

Social Security tax (6.2%): $5,000 × 6.2% = $310

Medicare tax (1.45%): $5,000 × 1.45% = $72.50

Total tax savings = $1,482.50

<u>Option 2: Claim the Child and Dependent Care Credit</u>

If Maria does not use a DCAP, she can claim the Child and Dependent Care Credit instead. Since her income is above $43,000, she qualifies for a 20% credit rate. With one child, the maximum amount of expenses she can claim is $3,000. So her Tax credit would be $600, which is $3,000 × 20%.

Health Insurance Premium Tax Credit (PTC)

If you purchase your health insurance through the marketplace, you may be eligible for the Premium Tax Credit. Income thresholds are higher for qualifying widowers with children than for single filers, which means you may be eligible for more assistance to help reduce your monthly premiums.

Retirement Savings Contributions Credit (Saver's Credit)

If your income is below $59,250 in 2025 and you contribute to a retirement plan, such as an IRA or 401(k), you may qualify for the Saver's Credit, worth up to $1,000. This credit reduces your tax liability and rewards you for saving during a challenging financial period.

Charitable Contributions and Deductions

If you itemize deductions, charitable donations can reduce your taxable income. One strategy is to group multiple years of donations into one tax year to exceed the standard deduction threshold. Under the new law, even if you do not itemize, you may deduct up to $1,000 in cash donations. This change allows more taxpayers to benefit from charitable giving while still using the standard deduction.

New Opportunities for 2025 (Qualifying Surviving Spouse)

Beginning in 2025, surviving spouses who meet the requirements to file as a qualifying widower can benefit from several temporary tax breaks introduced by the Tax One Big Beautiful Bill Act. These changes are designed to provide ongoing financial support during the transition period following the loss of a spouse.

Tax-Free Tips (Up to $25,000)

Widowed filers using this status can exclude up to $25,000 in tip income from federal taxes each year from 2025 through 2028. This can be especially helpful for those working in tipped positions while supporting children.

Overtime Deduction (Up to $12,500)

You can deduct up to $12,500 in qualified overtime wages from your taxable income. The deduction begins to phase out once your MAGI exceeds $150,000.

Expanded SALT Deduction Cap ($40,000)

The SALT deduction cap has increased to $40,000 for qualifying surviving spouses, matching the limit for married couples filing jointly. The cap begins to phase out once MAGI exceeds $500,000, and the deduction cannot be less than the original minimum of $10,000. This expanded cap is set to remain in effect through 2029 and will revert to earlier levels in 2030.

Car Loan Interest Deduction (Up to $10,000)

Interest on new personal-use car loans is now deductible, up to $10,000, for vehicles purchased between 2025 and 2028. To qualify, the car must be brand new, assembled in the United States, and financed with a first-lien secured loan. The vehicle also must be used strictly for personal purposes and not for business activities.

Senior Deduction ($6,000)

If you are sixty-five or older and your MAGI is under $75,000, you may qualify for an extra $6,000 deduction through 2029, provided you meet the eligibility criteria.

Withholding and Estimated Payments

It is essential to reassess your tax withholding and estimated payments after the death of a spouse. Changes in income or shifting household expenses can alter your tax obligations.

Example: Anita's husband passed in 2023. She mistakenly filed as Single in 2024, even though she met all the criteria for a Qualifying Widow(er). She missed out on valuable tax benefits.

Fortunately, she was able to file an amended return using Form 1040-X to correct her status and claim the correct refund.

Transitioning from MFJ to Qualifying Widow(er)

In the year of your spouse's death, you generally file using Married Filing Jointly. For the next two years, if eligible, you can file as a Qualifying Widow(er). After that, you may qualify for Head of Household if your child remains a dependent and resides with you.

Example: James lost his wife in 2022 and is raising their sixteen-year-old daughter. In 2023 and 2024, he filed as a Qualifying Widower. However, in 2025, since it's beyond the two-year limit, he must switch to Head of Household as long as his daughter continues to live with him and he provides more than half of the household support.

Maintaining Proper Documentation

Keep records such as your spouse's death certificate, documents proving child residency and support, and receipts for household expenses. This will help verify your filing status and ensure smooth processing of your tax return.

Comparison with Head of Household

Once the two-year Qualifying Widow(er) period ends, consider whether you qualify for Head of Household. It offers a higher standard deduction and better brackets than Single but has its own set of requirements for dependents and household costs.

Common Mistakes to Avoid

- Filing as Single instead of using Qualifying Widow(er) status when eligible
- Missing out on child-related tax credits

- Failing to adjust tax withholding after a spouse's death
- Assuming the status lasts more than two years

Tax Strategy Checklist

- Confirm that your spouse passed away in either of the two previous tax years.
- Ensure you have not remarried before the end of the current tax year.
- Verify that you have a dependent child or stepchild who lived with you for more than half the year.
- Confirm you paid more than half the cost of maintaining the household for the year.
- File using the Qualifying Widow(er) status to receive the same tax brackets and standard deduction as Married Filing Jointly.
- Claim eligible dependents and qualify for credits like the Child Tax Credit and education credits.
- Reevaluate your tax withholding using the IRS Withholding Estimator (www.irs.gov/W4app).
- Keep documentation such as your spouse's death certificate, dependent care expenses, and housing costs.
- Plan for the transition after two years to Head of Household or Single filing status.
- Avoid common mistakes, such as filing as Single too soon or forgetting to claim eligible credits.

Final Thoughts

This filing status offers meaningful financial relief during a difficult time. Taking advantage of the broader brackets, higher standard deduction, and available tax credits can ease the transition for both you and your children.

Chapter Ten
Tax Planning for Side Hustles and RSUs

Most of the tax strategies discussed so far focus on deferring tax liabilities with the expectation that your tax rate will be lower in retirement. While this approach can be effective, it has its limits, especially for high-earning W-2 employees who expect to maintain or increase their income over time. That's why building additional income streams, such as a side hustle or equity compensation, is not only a smart financial move but also opens the door to more flexible and powerful tax planning strategies. Side hustles and restricted stock units (RSUs) are increasingly common sources of income for W-2 earners. Whether you're freelancing, consulting, running a small online business, driving for a rideshare service, or receiving RSUs from your employer, it is crucial to understand how these income sources are taxed and how to plan around them. Proactive tax planning in these areas can help reduce your overall tax burden, create opportunities for deductions typically reserved for business owners, and provide more control over how and when you report income. In the following chapters, we will examine how W-2 earners can maximize their side income and equity compensation, both to reduce their tax burden today and to build long-term wealth.

Side Hustle Income and Self-Employment Taxes

If you earn income outside of your W-2 job, whether from freelancing, consulting, rideshare driving, or selling goods online, you are considered self-employed for tax purposes. Even small amounts of income are subject to self-employment tax, which covers both the employer and employee portions of Social Security and Medicare taxes. In 2025, if your net self-employment earnings are $400 or more, you are required to file a tax return and pay self-employment tax in addition to regular income tax. You must report this income on Schedule C and may also need to file Schedule SE to calculate the self-employment tax.

For example, Jessica earns $6,000 a year doing weekend photography. She reports the income on Schedule C and owes self-employment tax; however, she can also deduct business-related expenses, such as camera equipment, editing software, website hosting, and mileage. These deductions reduce her taxable income, helping to offset the added tax burden.

High-income W-2 earners with side hustles can significantly benefit from understanding how self-employment works. A side business provides access to tax-saving opportunities that are not available through W-2 income alone. These include the home office deduction, Section 179 depreciation for business equipment, deductions for health insurance premiums, and the ability to contribute to solo retirement plans such as a SEP IRA or Solo 401(k). By keeping detailed records, tracking all business expenses, and making quarterly estimated tax payments, you can reduce your overall tax bill and take greater control over how and when you pay taxes.

Because taxes aren't automatically withheld from side hustle income, you may need to make quarterly estimated tax payments to avoid penalties. Use the IRS Form 1040-ES to calculate how much to pay each quarter or talk to a tax professional.

Key Deductions for Side Hustles

W-2 earners who operate a side business may qualify for several powerful tax deductions typically available to self-employed individuals, including the Qualified Business Income (QBI) deduction and bonus depreciation. These provisions were established under the Tax Cuts and Jobs Act and can result in significant tax savings when utilized correctly.

The Qualified Business Income (QBI) deduction, also known as the Section 199A deduction, allows eligible sole proprietors and pass-through business owners, including side hustlers filing a Schedule C, to deduct up to 20% of their qualified business income. This deduction applies regardless of whether the taxpayer itemizes and is calculated after business expenses have been deducted. Under the new law, the QBI deduction has been made permanent, and income thresholds have been expanded. The phase-in and phase-out ranges for single filers are $75,000 to $95,000, and for joint filers, they are $150,000 to $190,000. A new minimum deduction of $400 is also available for those with at least $1,000 of QBI from active participation in a trade or business. For example, if Jasmine earns $25,000 in net income from freelance writing in addition to her W-2 job, she may be able to deduct up to $5,000 (20%) of this amount, thereby lowering her taxable income. Limitations based on income and business type still apply, so working with a tax professional is recommended.

Tax Pro Tip: Even small side hustles qualify for the 20% Qualified Business Income (QBI) deduction, as long as your income is under the phaseout limits.

Another powerful strategy is bonus depreciation, which allows businesses to immediately deduct 100% of the cost of eligible property placed in service after January 19th, 2025. The One Big Beautiful Bill Act (OBBBA) makes this 100% deduction permanent for most qualifying assets, reversing the previously scheduled phase-down. Eligible property includes tangible personal assets with a recovery period of twenty years or less, such as computers, cameras, office furniture, and certain vehicles. It also applies to specified media productions and, temporarily, to specific nonresidential real property used in manufacturing or refining. For instance, Aaron, a part-time videographer, buys

$5,000 worth of camera gear for client work. With the updated bonus depreciation rule, he can deduct the entire $5,000 in the same year, providing immediate tax savings.

For W-2 earners, the key is to keep business activity separate and well-documented. You must be operating a legitimate business with the intention of making a profit. By taking advantage of QBI, bonus depreciation, and other self-employment deductions like home office expenses and professional software, a side hustle can reduce your total tax liability and open the door to more flexible and efficient tax planning.

Two additional deductions that can offer meaningful savings for W-2 earners with a side hustle are home office expenses and mileage or vehicle-related deductions. If you use a portion of your home regularly and exclusively for business, you may qualify for the home office deduction. This includes a share of rent or mortgage interest, utilities, insurance, and repairs, based on the percentage of your home used for business. The IRS also offers a simplified option of $5 per square foot, up to 300 square feet. For example, Sarah teaches virtual fitness classes from a dedicated 120-square-foot room in her apartment. She can claim a $600 deduction under the simplified method or potentially more under the regular method by allocating a portion of her housing expenses to her office space.

If your side hustle requires driving, for client meetings, deliveries, or transporting gear, you can deduct vehicle expenses. The IRS allows two methods: the standard mileage rate (67 cents per mile in 2024, adjusted annually) or actual expenses, which include gas, maintenance, insurance, and depreciation. For example, Kevin delivers food part-time and drives 4,000 business miles annually. Using the standard mileage method, he could deduct $2,680, directly reducing his taxable self-employment income. To qualify, you must maintain detailed mileage logs and keep them separate for personal and business use. Both home office and vehicle deductions are subject to strict IRS rules, so proper documentation is key to defending these claims and maximizing your tax benefits.

Turn Family Help into Tax Deductions: Hiring Your Kids in Your Side Hustle

W-2 earners with a side hustle can hire their children to work in the business, which can create meaningful tax benefits if done correctly. If the child performs legitimate work appropriate for their age—such as managing social media, organizing inventory, or helping with administrative tasks—the wages paid are deductible as a business expense on Schedule C, reducing the parent's taxable business income. For sole proprietorships or single-member LLCs taxed as disregarded entities, wages paid to children under age eighteen are not subject to Social Security or Medicare taxes, and children under twenty-one are exempt from federal unemployment tax. If the child has no other income, they can earn up to the standard deduction amount ($15,750 in 2025) without owing federal income tax. For example, Mark owns a part-time photography business and hires his sixteen-year-old daughter to assist with editing and client scheduling. He pays her $5,000, which is fully deductible to him and tax-free to her. This strategy shifts income to a lower tax bracket while keeping money in the family. Still, it must be appropriately documented with time logs, a job description, and reasonable wages for the work performed.

Retirement Planning for Side Hustlers

Earning income from a side hustle gives you access to retirement savings options that are not available through W-2 income alone. If your side business has net earnings, you can contribute to several types of retirement accounts designed for the self-employed. One option is a SEP IRA, which allows you to contribute up to 25% of your net self-employment income, up to a maximum of $69,000 in 2025. Another powerful option is a Solo 401(k), which lets you contribute both as the employee and the employer. This means you can make a salary deferral of up to $23,500 (or $31,000 if you're fifty or older), plus an additional profit-sharing contribution of up to 25% of net earnings, all within the same $69,000 cap.

You can also contribute to a Traditional or Roth IRA using your total earned income from both your job and your business. Even small contributions can grow significantly over time through compounding. For example, Nora earns $15,000 from freelance writing in addition to her full-time job. She opens a Solo 401(k) and contributes $5,000 from her business income, reducing her taxable income and boosting her retirement savings. Whether you're freelancing occasionally or running a steady side business, these accounts can help you turn extra income into long-term financial security.

Understanding and Managing RSUs (Restricted Stock Units)

Restricted Stock Units (RSUs) are a type of equity compensation commonly offered by employers. You don't pay tax when RSUs are granted, but you are taxed when they vest. At vesting, the fair market value of the shares is treated as ordinary income and included in your W-2. For example, if 100 RSUs vest when the share price is $50, you will recognize $5,000 of income. Employers typically withhold taxes at the time of vesting, but the default federal withholding rate is 22%. If you are in a higher tax bracket, this may not cover your full tax liability and could result in a balance due when you file.

To manage the tax impact of RSUs, consider several strategies. First, review your withholding. If you fall into the 32% or 35% bracket, supplemental withholding at 22% may be too low. Making estimated tax payments or adjusting your W-2 withholding can help prevent underpayment penalties. Second, decide whether to sell shares immediately to cover the tax or hold them. Selling right away can help reduce exposure to market fluctuations and ensure you have sufficient funds to cover taxes. Holding the shares offers potential upside but also increases investment risk. If you hold shares after vesting and sell them later at a higher price, the gain is taxed as a capital gain. This gain is short-term if the shares are held for less than a year and long-term if held for one year or more. For example, Leah receives RSUs worth $10,000. If she holds them and the value rises to $15,000, she will owe capital gains tax on the $5,000 increase when she sells.

Common pitfalls include underestimating the tax impact of vested RSUs, holding too much company stock, which concentrates investment risk, and relying solely on the default tax withholding. Reviewing your tax bracket, tracking your vesting schedule, and planning can help you avoid surprises and use your RSUs as part of a broader financial strategy.

Watch Out: Restricted Stock Units (RSUs) are taxed as ordinary income when they vest. Plan ahead for the tax hit, especially if large grants push you into a higher bracket.

Checklist: Tax Planning for Side Hustles and RSUs

- Track all side hustle income and expenses using a spreadsheet or accounting app.
- Confirm whether your side hustle income exceeds $400 (if so, file Schedule C).
- Estimate self-employment tax and include it in your quarterly tax payments.
- Submit quarterly estimated tax payments using Form 1040-ES or IRS.gov.
- Keep detailed records of business-related expenses, including home office, mileage, internet, supplies, and other relevant costs.

- Open and fund a SEP IRA, Solo 401(k), or Traditional/Roth IRA using side hustle income.

- Check your RSU vesting schedule and understand your employer's tax withholding rate.

- Calculate whether RSU withholding (typically 22%) is sufficient for your tax bracket.

- Decide whether to sell RSU shares immediately (Sell-to-Cover) or hold for potential gains.

- Monitor for overconcentration in employer stock and rebalance your portfolio as needed.

- Track RSU transactions and include them when preparing your tax return.

- Review your Form W-4 or increase estimated payments to offset RSU-related taxes.

- Consult with a tax professional to optimize deductions for your side hustle and RSU strategies.

Final Thoughts on Side Hustles and RSUs

Side hustles and RSUs can offer powerful tax planning opportunities for W-2 earners, but they are not the right fit for everyone. Some may not have the time or interest to manage a side business, while others may not receive equity compensation from their employer. That said, for those who do have access to these income sources, the tax benefits can be substantial. A side hustle opens the door to deductions, business-related strategies, and retirement options that are not available through a regular job alone. RSUs can build wealth over time, especially when paired with smart planning around withholding and capital gains. To make the most of either, it's important to track income and expenses carefully, set aside funds for taxes, and work with a tax professional who understands your complete financial picture. With the right approach, both side income and equity compensation can become valuable tools for lowering your tax burden and increasing long-term financial stability.

Chapter Eleven
Maximizing Retirement Contributions

Planning for retirement is one of the most important financial goals for any W-2 earner. While Social Security may provide a foundation, it is rarely enough to maintain your current lifestyle. Which is why building personal retirement savings is essential, and fortunately, the tax code offers several ways to do that efficiently.

This chapter is designed to help you understand how to use employer-sponsored plans, IRAs, HSAs, and other tax-advantaged accounts to your benefit. Whether you are just starting or nearing retirement, these strategies can reduce your current tax bill, grow your wealth over time, and position you for long-term financial independence.

We will walk you through each primary type of retirement account available to W-2 employees, explain the tax advantages, and provide real-life examples to make the concepts easier to apply. You will also learn how to avoid common mistakes, optimize your contributions, and use credits and catch-up provisions to your advantage. Regardless of your income or life stage, there is likely a retirement strategy that can help you lower your taxes and increase your savings. Let's explore how.

Traditional 401(k) Plans

Traditional 401(k) contributions are made with pre-tax dollars, which reduces your current taxable income and allows for tax-deferred growth until retirement.

Example: Sarah, a thirty-five-year-old project manager, earns $95,000 a year. She contributes $20,000 to her traditional 401(k). By doing so, she lowers her taxable income to $75,000, which saves her approximately $4,400 in federal taxes, assuming she is in the 22% tax bracket.

The contribution limit for 2025 is $23,500, or $31,000 if you are age fifty or older. For workers aged sixty through sixty-three, the Secure 2.0 Act allows an additional catch-up contribution, bringing the deferral limit to $34,750. If your employer offers a 401(k) plan, you can also contribute on your own behalf. The combined employee and employer contribution limit is $70,000, or $77,500 if you are age fifty or older, and $81,250 if you are between sixty and sixty-three years old. For example, if you earn $100,000 and contribute $23,500 to your 401(k), your taxable income drops to $76,500, and your employer may add even more to help you reach the overall maximum.

Quick Math Example: Contributing $10,000 to a traditional 401(k) while in the 24% bracket reduces your federal income tax bill by about $2,400.

Roth 401(k) Plans

Roth 401(k) contributions are made with after-tax dollars. While you pay taxes now, qualified withdrawals in retirement are completely tax-free.

Example: Kevin is thirty and expects to be in a much higher tax bracket later in life. He chooses to contribute $10,000 to a Roth 401(k) this year. Though he pays taxes on the $10,000 now, he will pay no tax on it or its growth when he withdraws it in retirement, potentially saving tens of thousands in future taxes.

Recent law changes require that specific employer contributions, such as matching and non-elective contributions, be allocated to the Roth portion of your account if your plan allows it. This means you may end up with a mix of Traditional and Roth money, even if you only chose one type for your contributions.

403(b) Plans (For Nonprofits, Schools, and Hospitals)

A 403(b) plan is essentially the nonprofit sector's version of the 401(k). Teachers, hospital staff, clergy, and other employees of nonprofits or public schools often have access to this plan. The contribution limits are the same as a 401(k): $23,500 for 2025, or $31,000 if age fifty or older. The total combined limit, including employer contributions, is $69,000.

A unique feature of 403(b) plans is the fifteen-year service catch-up rule. If you have worked for the same qualified employer for at least fifteen years, you may be allowed to contribute up to an additional $3,000 per year, up to a lifetime maximum of $15,000. This is in addition to the standard age fifty catch-up.

403(b) contributions can be made in either a Traditional (pre-tax) or Roth (after-tax) format, which allows for tax reduction now or tax-free withdrawals later.

Example: Maria, a teacher earning $70,000, contributes $18,000 to her 403(b) retirement plan. Because she qualifies for the fifteen-year service rule, she contributes an additional $3,000, bringing her total contribution to $21,000. This reduces her taxable income to $49,000, saving her about $4,620 in federal taxes at a 22% marginal rate.

457(b) Plans (For State and Local Government Workers)

A 457(b) plan is available to many state and local government employees, as well as certain nonprofit workers. Similar to a 401(k) or 403(b), you can defer up to $23,500 in 2025, or $31,000 if you are fifty or older.

The key advantage is that 457(b) contributions do not count against your 401(k) or 403(b) limit. If you are eligible for both a

403(b) and a 457(b), you can contribute the maximum amount to each, potentially deferring up to $47,000 per year (more with catch-up contributions).

Another unique benefit: Withdrawals from a 457(b) are not subject to the 10% early withdrawal penalty if you separate from your employer, regardless of age. This makes the 457(b) one of the most flexible retirement accounts for public employees.

Example: James, a firefighter, earns $80,000 per year. He contributes $20,000 to his 457(b) plan and an additional $20,000 to his 403(b) plan. Combined, he saves $40,000 for retirement in one year and reduces his taxable income to $40,000, resulting in a significant upfront tax benefit.

Comparison of 401(k), 403(b), and 457(b) Plans (2025)

Feature	401(k)	403(b)	457(b)
Who Can Use It	Private-sector employees	Employees of public schools, hospitals, nonprofits, and clergy	State and local government employees, some nonprofit workers
Employee Contribution Limit	$23,500	$23,500	$23,500
Catch-Up at Age 50+	+$7,500	+$7,500	+$7,500
Total Contribution Limit (Employee + Employer)	$70,000	$70,000	$70,000

Special Catch-Up Provision	None	Extra $3,000 per year if 15 years with the same employer (lifetime max $15,000)	"Double limit" in the 3 years before retirement age, may allow up to $47,000 in employee deferrals
Tax Treatment	Traditional (pre-tax) or Roth (after-tax), depending on employer plan	Traditional or Roth, depending on employer plan	Traditional or Roth, depending on employer plan
Early Withdrawal Penalty	10% penalty before age 59½ (with exceptions, such as Rule of 55)	10% penalty before age 59½ (with exceptions)	No 10% penalty if you separate from service, regardless of age
Employer Match	Common	Common, but less generous in some nonprofits	Less common
Best For	Private-sector workers with access to an employer plan	Teachers, healthcare workers, and nonprofit employees	Public employees who want penalty-free access to funds if they leave the employer

Example: Linda is a fifty-two-year-old public school principal who also qualifies for her state's 457(b) plan. Her salary is $95,000. She contributes the maximum of $23,500 to her 403(b), plus the $7,500 catch-up contribution, for a total of $31,000. She also contributes $23,500 to her 457(b) plan, plus the $7,500 catch-up contribution, for a total of $31,000. In total, Linda saves $62,000 in one year toward retirement, all while lowering her taxable income to $33,000. Because she is over fifty, she takes advantage of both catch-up contributions. Additionally, since she is in a 457(b) plan, she has penalty-free access to those funds if she retires or leaves her employer.

Traditional IRA Contributions

A Traditional IRA allows you to contribute pre-tax or after-tax dollars, with potential for tax-deferred growth until you withdraw funds in retirement. For 2025, the annual contribution limit is $7,000 if you're under age fifty and $8,000 if you're fifty or older, including the $1,000 catch-up amount. Whether your contributions are fully deductible depends on your income and whether a workplace retirement plan covers you or your spouse. For single filers covered by a workplace plan, the deduction phases out between $77,000 and $87,000 of modified adjusted gross income (MAGI). For married couples filing jointly, where the contributing spouse is covered, the phase-out range is $123,000 to $143,000. If only the non-covered spouse contributes, the phase-out range is $230,000 to $240,000. Married couples can contribute to an IRA on behalf of a non-working spouse, effectively doubling retirement savings. This is especially useful for households with a stay-at-home parent. Traditional IRAs may be a good fit for earners who expect to be in a lower tax bracket during retirement, as contributions may reduce current taxable income.

Example: Dana, age forty-five, earns $65,000 and is not covered by a workplace plan. She contributes $7,000 to a Traditional IRA and qualifies for the full deduction, which lowers her taxable income and saves approximately $1,540 in federal taxes at a 22% marginal rate.

Roth IRA Contributions

A Roth IRA is a retirement account that allows you to contribute after-tax dollars and enjoy tax-free growth and tax-free withdrawals in retirement, provided certain conditions are met. For 2025, the annual contribution limit is $7,000 if you're under age fifty, and $8,000 if you're fifty or older, thanks to the $1,000 catch-up contribution; however, your ability to contribute phases out based on your modified adjusted gross income (MAGI). For single filers in 2025, the phase-out range is $146,000 to $161,000; for married couples filing jointly, it's $230,000 to $240,000. If your income exceeds these limits, you may not be able to contribute directly to a Roth IRA, though a backdoor Roth IRA strategy may still be available. Roth IRAs are especially attractive for younger earners or those expecting to be in a higher tax bracket in retirement, as the upfront tax payment can lead to greater tax savings in the long run.

Roth Conversions and the Backdoor Roth IRA Strategy

Roth conversions can be a powerful tax planning tool for W-2 earners, especially in years when your income is lower or when you exceed the income limits for direct Roth IRA contributions. A Roth conversion allows you to move funds from a Traditional IRA or 401(k) into a Roth IRA. You pay tax on the converted amount in the year of the transfer, but future growth and qualified withdrawals are tax-free.

This strategy can be beneficial during lower-income years. For example, Emily takes a career break and expects her income to decrease significantly. She converts $20,000 from her Traditional IRA to a Roth IRA while in the 12% tax bracket, paying just $2,400 in tax now and avoiding higher taxes on future withdrawals.

For high-income earners who are not eligible to contribute directly to a Roth IRA, a backdoor Roth IRA offers a workaround. In 2025, single filers with a modified adjusted gross income (MAGI) exceeding $161,000 and joint filers with a MAGI exceeding $240,000 are not eligible to make direct Roth contributions. However, they can contribute to a Traditional IRA (non-deductible) and then convert those funds to a Roth IRA. This is known as the backdoor Roth strategy. One key rule to understand is the IRS pro rata rule, which requires you to factor in all pre-tax IRA balances when calculating the taxable portion of the conversion. To minimize taxes, many use this strategy only when they have no other pre-tax IRA balances or after rolling those balances into an employer-sponsored plan, such as a 401(k).

Whether you're managing your tax brackets through timing or using the backdoor method to bypass income limits, Roth conversions can be an effective way to build tax-free retirement savings.

Health Savings Account (HSA) as a Retirement Tool

Using a Health Savings Account (HSA) as a retirement strategy offers one of the most tax-efficient ways to build long-term wealth. Suppose you are enrolled in a high-deductible health plan (HDHP). In that case, you can contribute up to $4,300 for self-only coverage or $8,550 for family coverage in 2025, with an additional $1,000 catch-up contribution if you are fifty-five or older. Contributions reduce your taxable income, the funds grow tax-free, and qualified medical withdrawals are also tax-free, giving HSAs a triple tax advantage. Unlike FSAs, the funds roll over indefinitely and can be invested in a variety of assets. A smart strategy is to pay for current medical expenses out of pocket, allowing your HSA to grow untouched and compound over time. After age sixty-five, you can withdraw funds for any purpose without penalty. Non-medical withdrawals are taxed as ordinary income. This makes the HSA a flexible backup to your retirement accounts, with the added benefit of covering future healthcare costs tax-free.

Example: Jordan is enrolled in a high-deductible health plan and contributes the full $4,150 into an HSA in 2025. He uses $1,500 for qualified medical expenses and invests the remaining $2,650. For twenty years, the invested amount grows tax-free and can be withdrawn tax-free for future healthcare expenses.

SEP IRA and Solo 401(k) for Side Hustlers

For W-2 earners with a side hustle, contributing to a SEP IRA or Solo 401(k) is a smart tax strategy that can significantly increase retirement savings while reducing taxable income. A SEP IRA allows you to contribute up to 25% of your net self-employment income, with a maximum of $69,000 in 2025. It is simple to set up and has no annual filing requirements, making it ideal for sole proprietors or freelancers with variable income. A Solo 401(k) is another strong option for self-employed individuals with no employees other than a spouse. In 2025, you can contribute up to $23,500 as the employee plus up to 25% of net self-employment income as the employer, for a total of $69,000. If you are fifty or older, you can make an additional $7,500 catch-up contribution. Solo 401(k)s also allow Roth contributions and offer loan provisions, which SEP IRAs do not. These plans enable side hustlers to build retirement savings beyond workplace plans and utilize their business income to achieve substantial tax-deferred or tax-free growth.

Saver's Credit

The Saver's Credit is a valuable but often overlooked tax strategy for low to moderate-income earners who contribute to a retirement account. Also known as the Retirement Savings Contributions Credit, it provides a tax credit of up to $1,000 ($2,000 for married couples filing jointly) based on your contributions to an IRA, 401(k), or other qualified retirement plans. In 2025, the credit is available to single filers with an adjusted gross income (AGI) of up to $38,250, heads of household with an AGI of up to $57,375, and joint filers with an AGI of up to $76,500. The credit rate, 10%, 20%, or 50%, depends on your income and filing status. Unlike a deduction, this credit directly reduces the amount of tax you owe. To qualify, you must be at least eighteen years old, not claimed as a dependent, and not a full-time student. W-2 eligible earners can benefit by reducing their tax bill while building retirement savings at the same time.

Employer Matching and Vesting Schedules

Many employers offer to match a portion of your 401(k) contributions, essentially providing free money to add to your retirement savings. Taking full advantage of this match is one of the most effective tax strategies for W-2 earners. Your contributions reduce your taxable income, and the employer match grows tax-deferred, helping you build retirement wealth while lowering your tax burden. To get the full benefit, contribute at least enough to receive the maximum match offered by your employer. It's also important to understand your plan's vesting schedule, which determines when you fully own the employer's contributions. If you leave the company before you're fully vested, you could lose part of that match. Understanding vesting terms can help you make more informed career decisions and retain a greater portion of your long-term savings.

Avoiding Early Withdrawal Penalties

Taking money out of retirement accounts before age 59½ usually triggers a 10% early withdrawal penalty, in addition to regular income tax. This applies to Traditional IRAs, 401(k)s, and similar tax-deferred plans. However, several exceptions can help you access funds without the penalty if needed. For example, up to $10,000 can be withdrawn penalty-free from a Traditional IRA for a first-time home purchase. Other exceptions include qualified higher education expenses, certain medical costs that exceed 7.5% of your adjusted gross income, permanent disability, and health insurance premiums while unemployed. For 401(k) plans, separation from service at age fifty-five or older (often referred to as the "Rule of 55") allows penalty-free withdrawals if you leave your job. Additionally, both IRAs and 401(k)s allow penalty-free withdrawals through Substantially Equal Periodic Payments (SEPP), though this option comes with strict rules and long-term commitment. While these exceptions can be helpful in a pinch, they reduce your retirement savings, so they should be considered only after evaluating other options. Planning and understanding the rules can help you avoid costly penalties while maintaining your long-term goals.

Checklist for Maximizing Retirement Contributions

- Contribute to a Traditional or Roth 401(k): The 2025 limit is $23,500, or $31,000 if you are age fifty or older, thanks to the $7,500 catch-up contribution.

- Evaluate Roth 401(k) vs. Traditional 401(k): Consider your current and expected future tax brackets. Roth 401(k)s offer tax-free withdrawals, while Traditional 401(k)s provide upfront tax deductions.

- Use a 403(b) if You Work in Education, Healthcare, or Nonprofits: Same contribution limits as a 401(k). If you have 15 years of service with the same employer, check if you qualify for the special $3,000 annual service-based catch-up contribution.

- Take Advantage of a 457(b) if You Are a Public Employee: Contribution limits are separate from your 401(k) or 403(b). You can maximize both in the same year. Withdrawals after leaving your job are not subject to the 10% early penalty.

- Make Traditional IRA Contributions: You can contribute up to $7,000 in 2025, or $8,000 if you are age 50 or older. Deductibility depends on income and whether you have access to a workplace retirement plan.

- Check Roth IRA Eligibility: In 2025, the ability to contribute phases out for single filers with MAGI between $146,000 and $161,000, and for married couples filing jointly between $230,000 and $240,000.

- Consider a Backdoor Roth IRA: If you are over the income limit, contribute to a non-deductible Traditional IRA and convert to a Roth IRA. Watch for the pro rata rule.

- Fund an HSA if Enrolled in a High-Deductible Health Plan: The 2025 HSA contribution limit is $4,300 for individuals and $8,550 for families. Those 55 or older can contribute an extra $1,000.

- Open a SEP IRA or Solo 401(k) for Side Income: You can contribute up to $70,000 in 2025 (plus $7,500 catch-up in a Solo 401(k) if age 50 or older), depending on your net self-employment income.

- Make Spousal IRA Contributions: If one spouse has little or no income, the working spouse can contribute to a spousal IRA under the same annual limits.

- Claim the Saver's Credit if Eligible: In 2025, the credit is available to single filers with AGI up to $38,250, heads of household up to $57,375, and joint filers up to $76,500.

- Maximize Catch-Up Contributions: If you are 50 or older, take advantage of higher contribution limits across 401(k), 403(b), 457(b), IRA, HSA, and Solo 401(k) plans.

- Contribute Enough to Receive the Full Employer Match: Don't leave free money on the table. Check your plan's match formula and contribute accordingly.

- Review Your Plan's Vesting Schedule: Know when employer contributions become yours. Leaving a job too early may result in forfeiting part of your match contribution.

- Time Roth Conversions for Low-Income Years: Converting Traditional IRA or 401(k) funds to a Roth can be more tax-efficient when you are in a lower tax bracket.

- Avoid Early Withdrawal Penalties: Most retirement accounts impose a 10% penalty before age 59½. Know the exceptions for home buying, education, health costs, and separation from service after age 55 (for 401(k)s). Withdrawals from 457(b) plans are exempt from this penalty if you leave your employer.

Final Thoughts on Retirement Contributions

Consistent contributions, especially with tax-smart strategies, can significantly boost your retirement readiness. Understand the rules, stay within limits, and maximize available tax benefits every year. If you are in the private sector, your focus may be on the 401(k) and IRA options. If you work in education, healthcare, or the government, you may have access to a 403(b) or 457(b) plan, which can be just as powerful. In some cases, you can contribute to both a 403(b) and a 457(b) in the same year, effectively doubling your retirement savings potential.

The key is to contribute enough to capture your employer match, use catch-up provisions if you are over fifty, and balance Traditional versus Roth contributions based on your current and expected future tax brackets. A little planning each year can add up to a much more secure and flexible retirement.

Chapter Twelve
Using FSAs, HSAs, and Dependent Care Accounts

As a W-2 earner, managing medical and childcare costs is a financial reality, but it also presents a tax-saving opportunity. Flexible Spending Accounts (FSAs), Health Savings Accounts (HSAs), and Dependent Care FSAs are employer-sponsored tools that can reduce your taxable income while helping you cover essential expenses. While these accounts are often overlooked or underutilized, when used strategically, they can generate thousands in tax savings each year. In this chapter, we'll break down each account type, how they work, and real-life examples to show how everyday employees can benefit.

What Is a Flexible Spending Account (FSA)?

A Flexible Spending Account (FSA) enables you to set aside pre-tax dollars to cover qualified medical expenses, thereby reducing your taxable income. For 2025, the annual contribution limit is $3,200. These funds can be used for expenses like copays, prescriptions, over-the-counter medications, and specific medical devices.

For example, Tasha, a teacher who typically spends $2,000 per year on healthcare, contributes that amount to her FSA, lowering her taxable income by the same amount and saving approximately $500 in taxes. The main benefit of an FSA is the immediate tax savings, but it comes with a catch: the "use-it-or-lose-it" rule. Any unused funds at the end of the plan year may be forfeited unless your employer offers a short grace period or allows a limited rollover. In Mark's case, he contributed $3,000 but only used $2,000, and because his employer didn't offer a rollover, he lost the remaining $1,000. To avoid this, it's essential to estimate your medical expenses carefully each year.

Watch Out: Most FSAs are "use it or lose it." If you don't spend the money in the plan year (or grace period), you forfeit it.

What Is a Health Savings Account (HSA)?

A Health Savings Account (HSA) is one of the most tax-efficient tools available for W-2 earners enrolled in a high-deductible health plan (HDHP). HSAs offer triple tax benefits: contributions reduce your taxable income, investments grow tax-free, and withdrawals for qualified medical expenses are also tax-free. In 2025, the contribution limit is $4,300 for individuals and $8,550 for families. If you are fifty-five or older, you can contribute an additional $1,000 as a catch-up contribution.

For example, Jasmine, age fifty-five, contributes $5,150 to her HSA—$4,150 plus the $1,000 catch-up—and uses $1,500 for dental surgery. The rest remains in the account, growing tax-free for future expenses, such as Medicare premiums or long-term care. HSAs differ from FSAs because the funds roll over from year to year and can be invested in a variety of assets. Carlos and his wife, both in their early fifties, contribute the full $8,300, and Carlos adds his $1,000 catch-up, reducing their taxable income by $9,300 and saving over $2,200 in taxes at a 24% rate. After age sixty-five, you can also withdraw funds for non-medical purposes without a penalty, though those withdrawals are taxed as ordinary income. This flexibility makes HSAs an excellent supplemental retirement account, especially for covering healthcare costs in later years.

What Is a Dependent Care FSA?

A Dependent Care Flexible Spending Account (FSA) enables working parents and caregivers to set aside up to $5,000 per household in pre-tax dollars annually to cover eligible dependent care expenses. This reduces your taxable income and can result in significant tax savings. In 2025, eligible expenses include daycare, preschool, summer day camps, and care for a dependent or spouse who is physically or mentally unable to care for themselves while you work.

For example, Angela and Sam contribute $4,500 to their Dependent Care FSA to cover daycare costs for their toddler, saving over $1,100 in taxes. Single dad Kevin utilizes his $5,000 Dependent Care FSA to cover after-school care for his ten-year-old daughter, thereby reducing other financial burdens. The Dependent Care FSA can also be used in conjunction with the Child and Dependent Care Tax Credit, although the same expenses cannot be claimed for both. For instance, Brian contributed the maximum $5,000 to his Dependent Care FSA and claimed the tax credit for additional qualified expenses, reducing his total tax bill by more than $2,000. Planning can help families maximize the benefits from both options.

Quick Math Example: Contributing $5,000 to a Dependent Care FSA saves about $1,100 in federal taxes if you're in the 22% bracket.

Comparison of FSAs, HSAs, and Dependent Care FSAs

Feature	FSA (Health)	HSA	Dependent Care FSA
Contribution Limit (2025)	$3,200	$4,150 (individual), $8,300 (family)	$5,000 per household
Catch-Up Contributions	Not allowed	$1,000 allowed if age 55 or older	Not allowed
Use-it-or-Lose-it Rule	Yes (with limited rollover or grace)	No	Yes
Rollover Allowed	Limited (up to $640 if offered)	Full rollover each year	No
Investment Option	No	Yes (can invest and grow tax-free)	No
Must Be Enrolled in HDHP	No	Yes	No
Funds Usable in Retirement	No	Yes (after age 65 for any purpose, taxable if non-medical)	No
Reduces FICA Taxes	Yes	No	Yes

Real-Life Planning Scenario

Teresa, age forty-two, is enrolled in a high-deductible health plan. She contributes $8,300 to her family HSA and plans to let it grow for future medical expenses in retirement. At the same time, she estimates $2,500 in medical costs for the year and contributes that amount to her employer's FSA instead of tapping into her HSA. She also contributes $5,000 to her Dependent Care FSA to cover preschool costs for her son. Together, these three strategies lower her taxable income by $15,800. Assuming Teresa is in the

22% federal tax bracket, she might save about $3,500 in federal income taxes.

Tax Pro Tip: If your employer offers both an HSA and an FSA, check whether it's a "limited purpose" FSA for dental and vision. Using both correctly maximizes your tax savings.

Common Mistakes to Avoid

- Forgetting to use FSA funds by the deadline, resulting in forfeited money
- Contributing to both an HSA and a general-purpose FSA (not allowed unless the FSA is limited purpose)
- Double-dipping by claiming dependent care expenses both in the FSA and on your tax return
- Choosing an HSA-eligible plan without understanding the higher deductible

Checklist: Maximizing FSAs, HSAs, and Dependent Care Accounts

- Confirm your eligibility for an FSA, HSA, or Dependent Care FSA through your employer or health plan.
- For FSAs, elect your annual contribution amount (up to $3,200 for 2025) during open enrollment.
- For HSAs, verify you are enrolled in a High-Deductible Health Plan (HDHP). Contribute up to $4,150 individually or $8,300 for families (plus $1,000 catch-up if over 55).
- For Dependent Care FSAs, elect up to $5,000 per household ($2,500 if MFS).
- Track eligible expenses: Keep receipts for copays, prescriptions, dental, vision, and dependent care.
- Use your account debit card or submit reimbursements with documentation.

- Monitor deadlines: Spend FSA funds before the plan year ends, or check if your plan has a grace period or rollover option.
- Review employer contributions and coordination rules if using multiple accounts.
- Avoid over-contribution: Stay within annual IRS limits to avoid penalties.
- Report HSA contributions and distributions on Form 8889 with your tax return.
- Coordinate Dependent Care FSA with the Child and Dependent Care Tax Credit if applicable.

Final Thoughts on FSAs, HSAs, and Dependent Care FSAs

These accounts offer some of the most effective tax-saving opportunities for employees. Used wisely, they can save thousands annually while providing for medical and childcare needs. Consult with your employer's HR department or a tax advisor to ensure you're maximizing these benefits.

Chapter Thirteen

Year-End Tax Planning and Life Events That Impact Your Taxes

For many W-2 earners, tax planning often feels like something that only occurs during tax filing season. But by then, the window for action has closed. The real opportunity to influence your tax bill appears in the final weeks of the calendar year. Year-end tax planning is one of the most powerful ways to take control of your finances, reduce your tax liability, and make smart choices that carry over into the new year. This chapter focuses on practical steps W-2 employees can take before December 31st, while also preparing for key life events that could significantly affect their taxes. Whether you're reviewing your paycheck after a raise, calculating how RSUs will impact your tax bracket, or navigating changes such as marriage, a new child, job transitions, or buying a home, understanding the tax implications and planning can make a significant difference.

Adjusting Withholding to Avoid Surprises

Review your Form W-4 by the end of the year to ensure you've withheld enough to cover your tax liability. Use the IRS Tax Withholding Estimator (www.irs.gov/W4app) to determine the correct amount. If you've received bonuses, vested RSUs, or changed jobs mid-year, your withholding may need to be updated to reflect your actual income.

Safe Harbor Rules to Avoid Penalties

To avoid an underpayment penalty, follow the IRS safe harbor rule: Pay at least 100% of your prior year's tax liability (or 110% if your AGI exceeded $150,000), or 90% of your current year's liability. If you're unsure, consider making a year-end estimated payment.

Harvesting Capital Losses

Selling underperforming investments before year-end can offset capital gains. You can deduct up to $3,000 of net capital losses against ordinary income, with excess carried forward to future years.

Timing Charitable Contributions

Charitable donations must be made by December 31st to be deductible for the current tax year. Donating appreciated assets can provide a full deduction and avoid capital gains tax.

Bunching Itemized Deductions

If your itemized deductions are close to the standard deduction ($15,750 for single, $31,500 for married filing jointly in 2025), consider bunching deductions like charitable gifts or medical procedures into one year to maximize their impact.

Maxing Out Retirement Contributions

Contribute the maximum to your 401(k) by year-end ($23,500 or $31,000 if age fifty or older). IRA contributions can be made until April 15th, but making contributions earlier helps avoid surprises and allows your savings to grow faster.

Using Up Flexible Spending Accounts (FSAs)

FSA funds often expire at the end of the year unless your plan includes a grace period or limited rollover. Use remaining funds on eligible medical expenses.

Deferring Income and Accelerating Expenses

If you control the timing of your income, consider delaying it until January if it will keep you in a lower tax bracket this year. Likewise, prepaying deductible expenses such as mortgage interest or business costs before December 31st can lower this year's taxable income.

Reviewing Estimated Payments and Credit Eligibility

Ensure your total withholding and estimated payments meet IRS thresholds. Consider a final estimated payment by January 15th if needed. Additionally, review eligibility for tax credits, such as the Child Tax Credit, Earned Income Tax Credit, and Saver's Credit.

Gathering Tax Documents Early

Collect W-2s, 1099s, donation receipts, and account statements in advance to ensure a smooth tax preparation process. Early preparation helps ensure accurate and timely filing.

Planning for Next Year's Changes

As you plan for next year, consider how significant life changes, such as marriage, a new child, a job switch, or homeownership, may impact your taxes. Update your W-4 and review benefit elections during open enrollment.

Marriage

Marriage changes your filing options. Most couples benefit from filing jointly, which offers broader tax brackets and higher deductions. However, if both spouses earn high incomes, the marriage penalty may apply. Update your W-4, evaluate whether to itemize deductions, and review eligibility for new tax credits.

Having or Adopting a Child

Children can lead to meaningful tax savings. You may qualify for the Child Tax Credit, Dependent Care Credit, and, if applicable, the Adoption Credit. Ensure that you apply for a Social Security number for each child. For special needs adoptions, you may be eligible for the full credit regardless of costs.

Changing Jobs

Job changes can affect withholding and trigger taxable income from severance, signing bonuses, or relocation packages. Be sure to update your W-4 and consider rolling over your 401(k) to avoid taxes on early withdrawals.

Buying a Home

Homeownership can change how you file your taxes. While many still use the standard deduction, itemizing may be worthwhile if mortgage interest, property taxes, and other deductions exceed the threshold. Save records for mortgage points, energy-efficient improvements, and closing costs.

IRS Reminder: To avoid penalties, use the IRS safe harbor rule: pay 100% of last year's tax (110% if you earned more than $150,000) through withholding or estimated payments.

Final Thoughts on Year-End Planning and Life Events

The end of the year offers W-2 earners a unique opportunity to shape their tax outcomes before the calendar turns. Combining year-end strategies with an understanding of how life events impact your tax profile enables you to be more proactive, maximize credits and deductions, and avoid surprises. Planning, adjusting withholding, and staying on top of changing circumstances can lead to lower taxes and better financial outcomes in both the short and long term.

Bonus Chapter

Advanced Tax Strategies for W-2 Earners for specialized, high-income taxpayers only

In this chapter, we'll dive deeper into advanced tax strategies for W-2 earners. These strategies are not one-size-fits-all and often require more careful planning, risk evaluation, and sometimes professional guidance. When implemented correctly, they can help reduce taxable income, increase long-term savings, and align with broader financial goals.

1. College Savings with 529 Plans

A 529 plan allows after-tax contributions to grow tax-free when used for qualified education expenses, such as tuition, room and board, and books. Some states also offer tax deductions or credits for contributions.

Example: Maria and Luis, a married couple with a combined income of $190,000, open a 529 account for their daughter. They contribute $500 monthly for thirteen years. Assuming a 6% average return, they accumulate over $120,000 in tax-free funds.

2. Permanent Life Insurance as a Retirement - High Fees, Suitable Only After Maxing all Other Retirement Options

Permanent life insurance, such as Whole Life or Indexed Universal Life (IUL), builds cash value over time. This cash value grows tax-deferred and can be accessed tax-free through policy loans. It's most beneficial after maxing out 401(k) and IRA contributions.

Example: James, a forty-two-year-old engineer earning $130,000, pays $10,000 annually into an IUL policy. After fifteen years, his cash value exceeds $160,000, which he accesses tax-free in retirement via policy loans.

3. Intangible Drilling Costs (IDCs) - High-Risk/Advanced

IDCs are deductible expenses related to oil and gas exploration. High-income W-2 earners who become general partners in drilling projects can deduct a significant portion of their investment in the year it is incurred.

Example: Tina invests $25,000 in a drilling partnership. She exceeds the 80% ($20,000) that qualifies as an IDC and is deductible. She reduces her taxable income from $220,000 to $200,000, saving over $7,000 in federal taxes.

4. Backdoor Roth IRA

A backdoor Roth IRA enables high-income earners to fund a Roth IRA by contributing to a non-deductible Traditional IRA and then converting it. This bypasses Roth income limits.

Example: Sarah earns $190,000 and is over the Roth IRA income limit. She contributes $7,000 to a non-deductible Traditional IRA and then converts it to a Roth IRA, allowing for tax-free growth.

5. Mega Backdoor Roth IRA

If your employer's 401(k) plan allows it, you can contribute after-tax dollars beyond the $23,500 or $31,000 limit (if over fifty years old) and convert them to a Roth 401(k). This can increase your total annual contribution to $70,000.

Example: Anna earns $180,000 and contributes $23,000 pre-tax plus $30,000 after-tax to her 401(k). She converts the after-tax portion to a Roth 401(k), allowing her to enjoy additional tax-free growth.

6. Tax-Loss Harvesting

This strategy involves selling investments at a loss to offset capital gains and reduce taxable income. Unused losses (up to $3,000) can offset ordinary income annually.

Example: Mark sells a stock for a $5,000 loss and uses it to offset a $5,000 capital gain from another investment. He avoids capital gains tax and carries forward any unused losses.

7. Donor-Advised Funds (DAFs)

A DAF allows you to contribute a large charitable donation in one year, take an immediate tax deduction, and distribute the funds to charities over time.

Example: Denise donates $25,000 to a donor-advised fund (DAF) in one year. She itemizes that year and takes the standard deduction in future years while still supporting her charities gradually.

8. Health Reimbursement Arrangements (HRAs) for Spouses

If your spouse owns a business, you may be eligible to be hired and reimbursed for medical expenses through an HRA. The business deducts the reimbursement, and you receive it tax-free.

Example: Lisa's husband owns a consulting business. He hires her and reimburses $10,000 in family medical costs through an HRA, saving over $2,000 in taxes.

9. Executive Bonus Plans and Restricted Property Trusts - High-Risk/Advanced

These insurance-based strategies provide tax-deferred savings and offer future tax-free distributions to high-income earners. They require working with a planner and a long-term commitment.

Example: Tom earns $400,000 and uses an executive bonus plan to fund a life insurance policy that will grow cash value and supplement his retirement income tax-free.

10. Investing in Municipal Bonds

Interest from municipal bonds is exempt from federal taxes and, in some cases, state taxes. This makes them attractive for those in high tax brackets seeking stable, tax-free income.

Example: John invests in a municipal bond yielding 4%. At a 35% tax bracket, that is equivalent to a 6.15% taxable yield.

11. Rental Property as a Tax Strategy

Owning a rental property can provide both long-term wealth and meaningful tax advantages. The IRS allows deductions for mortgage interest, property taxes, insurance, repairs, and depreciation. Depreciation is especially powerful because it is a non-cash expense that reduces taxable income, often creating paper losses even if the property generates positive cash flow.

If your modified adjusted gross income (MAGI) is below $100,000, you may deduct up to $25,000 of rental losses against W-2 income if you actively participate in managing the property. The benefit phases out between $100,000 and $150,000 of MAGI. Even if you cannot use the losses now, they carry forward and can offset rental profits or capital gains when you sell the property.

Example: John earns $120,000 in wages and buys a rental that generates $12,000 in rent. After expenses and depreciation, the property shows a $3,000 paper loss. Because his income exceeds $150,000, he cannot deduct the loss this year; however, it carries forward. When he sells the property for a $50,000 gain years later, the prior losses offset part of the taxable gain.

Advanced strategies, such as short-term rentals (Airbnb/VRBO), 1031 exchanges, and cost segregation, can further enhance tax benefits; however, they require more active involvement and professional guidance to be effective.

Watch Out: Strategies such as oil and gas drilling investments or permanent life insurance policies are high-risk and not suitable for most W-2 earners. Only pursue them after maxing out traditional accounts like 401(k)s, IRAs, and HSAs.

12. Timing and Bunching Deductions

By accelerating or delaying deductible expenses, you can bunch them into one year to surpass the standard deduction and itemize strategically.

Example: Rachel donates $15,000 in December instead of splitting the amount over two years. Combined with other deductions, she itemizes that year and takes the standard deduction the next.

13. Employer Fringe Benefits: Pick the Right Mix

Many employer benefits offer tax-preferred treatment. Examples:

- Group term life insurance (first $50,000 tax-free)
- Educational assistance (up to $5,250/year tax-free for tuition reimbursement)
- Legal services plans or identity theft coverage
- Transit or commuter benefits

Advanced Tax Strategies for W-2 Earners: Printable Checklist

- Open and fund a 529 Plan for children's education.
- Evaluate permanent life insurance as a supplemental retirement tool.
- Assess risk and eligibility before investing in oil & gas partnerships for IDC deductions.

- Make a non-deductible traditional IRA contribution and complete a backdoor Roth IRA conversion.

- Check if your 401(k) allows for Mega Backdoor Roth contributions.

- Review portfolio for tax-loss harvesting opportunities before year-end.

- Set up or contribute to a Donor-Advised Fund (DAF) for charitable giving.

- If your spouse owns a small business, explore setting up an HRA for family medical reimbursements.

- Consult a financial advisor about Executive Bonus Plans or Restricted Property Trusts.

- Invest in municipal bonds for tax-free interest income if in a high tax bracket.

- Explore rental property ownership as a tax-advantaged investment.

- Consider bunching deductions, such as medical expenses or charitable donations, into one year.

Final Thoughts

These strategies aren't for everyone, but they show what's possible when W-2 earners think beyond the basics. You don't need to own a business to take advantage of the tax code. With thoughtful planning and professional guidance, W-2 employees can access sophisticated tools to save on taxes and plan for the future.

Final Thoughts

Tax Planning Isn't Just for the Wealthy; Know More, Keep More

Too many W-2 earners mistakenly believe they are stuck with whatever tax bill arrives in April. That's only true if you wait until the end of the year to start thinking about your taxes.

This book has shown that good tax planning doesn't require owning a business or hiring a team of advisors. It takes awareness of your income, deductions, credits, and how everyday decisions, such as adjusting your W-4, choosing the right benefits, funding retirement accounts, or opening a 529 plan, can add up to thousands in savings. For those ready to take their tax planning to the next level, advanced strategies such as rental property ownership, backdoor Roth contributions, donor-advised funds, and municipal bonds can provide even more opportunities to reduce taxes and build wealth.

You now have a toolkit: one that covers the essentials, offers advanced moves, and helps you adapt as life changes. Use it. Review your paystub. Revisit your filing status. Ask better questions at work about your benefits. Determine whether real estate or other investments are suitable for your situation. Consult a CPA or tax professional when life becomes more complex.

Your tax return is more than a form; it reflects your financial choices. The more you understand it, the more money stays in your hands.

Your Next Step

Knowledge only pays off when you act on it. Pick one strategy from this book, whether it's adjusting your W-4, increasing your 401(k) contribution, opening a Roth IRA, or researching a rental property—and put it into motion this week. Even small steps compound over time, and the sooner you start, the more control you take over your financial future.

Acknowledgments

I would like to thank my editor, Ashley Emma, for her thoughtful feedback and meticulous attention to detail throughout this project. Her guidance helped shape this book into a clear and practical resource for readers.

I would also like to acknowledge my brother, Eustache Clerveaux, who reviewed the first draft and provided valuable suggestions that significantly improved both the clarity and flow of the chapters. His support and insight were a meaningful part of this process.

Finally, I am deeply grateful to my family and friends for their patience and encouragement as I balanced writing with work and family life. Their belief in this project kept me focused on finishing what I started.

Appendices

Appendix A: References

- IRS 2025 Tax Brackets: IRS Newsroom 2025 Bracket Update – Chapters 1, 2, 5, 6, 7, 8, 9, 13

- IRS Revenue Procedure 2024-40 (2025 Inflation Adjustments): IRS Rev. Proc. 2024-40 – Chapters 2, 3, 5, 6, 7, 8, 9, 13

- IRS Publication 501 (Filing Status, Standard Deduction): IRS Pub. 501 – Chapters 2, 5, 6, 7, 8, 9

- IRS Publication 503 (Child and Dependent Care Expenses): IRS Pub. 503 – Chapters 6, 8, 9, 12

- IRS Publication 505 (Withholding and Estimated Tax): IRS Pub. 505 – Chapters 1, 13

- IRS Publication 526 (Charitable Contributions): IRS Pub. 526 – Chapters 3, 5, 6, 7, 8, 9, 13, Bonus

- IRS Publication 550 (Investment Income): IRS Pub. 550 – Chapters 5, 6, 7, 8, 9, 10, 13

- IRS Publication 555 (Community Property): IRS Pub. 555 – Chapter 7

- IRS Publication 590-A (IRA Contributions): IRS Pub. 590-A – Chapters 5, 6, 7, 8, 9, 10, 11

- IRS Publication 969 (HSAs and Other Tax-Favored Accounts): IRS Pub. 969 – Chapters 5, 6, 7, 8, 9, 11, 12

- IRS Publication 970 (Education Credits): IRS Pub. 970 – Chapters 4, 5, 6, 7, 8, 9, 11

Appendix B: Index

About the Author

Julio Clerveaux is Vice President of Private Company Data at CreditRiskMonitor. He leads a team responsible for analyzing and maintaining financial information and proprietary risk scores for private companies. With over a decade of experience in financial and risk analysis, he has played a key role in delivering accurate and reliable credit risk insights.

Outside of his role at CreditRiskMonitor, Mr. Clerveaux is an Enrolled Agent (EA), a federally licensed tax professional authorized by the U.S. Department of the Treasury to represent taxpayers before the IRS. He earned this designation by passing a comprehensive three-part exam covering individual taxation, business taxation, and IRS representation procedures. With unlimited practice rights, he advises individuals and small business owners on effective tax strategies to minimize liability and improve financial outcomes. Julio is also a member of the National Association of Enrolled Agents and holds a Master of Business Administration.

Important Notice

The tax strategies and examples in this book are provided for general informational purposes only. Tax laws change, and individual situations vary. Before acting on any information in this book, consult a licensed tax professional who can advise you based on your specific facts and goals.

Made in the USA
Middletown, DE
30 November 2025

23533205R00077